Remain in His Love

90 DEVOTIONS TO HELP YOU DIG DEEP AND DRAW CLOSER TO GOD

DR. JACKIE GREENE

AUTHOR OF *PERMISSION TO LIVE FREE*

NELSON
BOOKS

An Imprint of Thomas Nelson

Remain in His Love

Published in Nashville, Tennessee, by Nelson Books, an imprint of Thomas Nelson. Nelson Books and Thomas Nelson are registered trademarks of HarperCollins Christian Publishing, Inc.

The author is represented by Alive Literary Agency, www.aliveliterary.com.

Thomas Nelson titles may be purchased in bulk for educational, business, fundraising, or sales promotional use. For information, please email SpecialMarkets@ThomasNelson.com.

Unless otherwise noted, Scripture quotations are taken from the Holy Bible, New Living Translation. Copyright © 1996, 2004, 2015 by Tyndale House Foundation. Used by permission of Tyndale House Publishers, Inc., Carol Stream, Illinois 60188. All rights reserved. Scripture quotations marked AMP are taken from the Amplified® Bible (AMP). Copyright © 2015 by The Lockman Foundation. Used by permission. www.lockman.org. Scripture quotations marked ESV are taken from the ESV® Bible (The Holy Bible, English Standard Version®). Copyright © 2001 by Crossway, a publishing ministry of Good News Publishers. Used by permission. All rights reserved. Scripture quotations marked KJV are taken from the King James Version. Public domain. Scripture quotations marked MSG are taken from *THE MESSAGE*. Copyright © 1993, 2002, 2018 by Eugene H. Peterson. Used by permission of NavPress. All rights reserved. Represented by Tyndale House Publishers, Inc. Scripture quotations marked NASB are taken from the New American Standard Bible®. Copyright © 1960, 1971, 1977, 1995 by The Lockman Foundation. Used by permission. All rights reserved. www.lockman.org. Scripture quotations marked NIV are taken from the Holy Bible, New International Version®, NIV®. Copyright © 1973, 1978, 1984, 2011 by Biblica, Inc.® Used by permission of Zondervan. All rights reserved worldwide. www.Zondervan.com. The "NIV" and "New International Version" are trademarks registered in the United States Patent and Trademark Office by Biblica, Inc.® Scripture quotations marked NKJV are taken from the New King James Version.® Copyright © 1982 by Thomas Nelson. Used by permission. All rights reserved.

Any internet addresses, phone numbers, or company or product information printed in this book are offered as a resource and are not intended in any way to be or to imply an endorsement by Thomas Nelson, nor does Thomas Nelson vouch for the existence, content, or services of these sites, phone numbers, companies, or products beyond the life of this book.

Library of Congress Cataloging-in-Publication Data

Names: Greene, Jackie, 1987- author.
Title: Remain in His love : 90 devotions to help you dig deep and draw closer to God / Dr. Jackie Greene.
Description: Nashville, Tennessee : Nelson Books, [2024] | Includes bibliographical references. | Summary: "Come on a 90-day journey with pastor, Bible teacher, and author Dr. Jackie Greene as she encourages you to dig deep into His Word and discover and enjoy a love that never ends"-- Provided by publisher.
Identifiers: LCCN 2024009195 (print) | LCCN 2024009196 (ebook) | ISBN 9781400241934 (hardcover) | ISBN 9781400241927 (ebook)
Subjects: LCSH: Love--Religious aspects--Christianity. | Love--Biblical teaching.
Classification: LCC BS680.L64 G744 2024 (print) | LCC BS680.L64 (ebook) | DDC 242--dc23/eng/20240326
LC record available at https://lccn.loc.gov/2024009195
LC ebook record available at https://lccn.loc.gov/2024009196

Printed in the United States of America

24 25 26 27 28 LBC 5 4 3 2 1

I dedicate this devotional to my Abba Father, the one I affectionately call Daddy. Years ago I fervently prayed for the stick-to-it-ness to fill journals through personal time spent with You. This devotional stands as a tangible answer to that prayer. Your love so wide and long and high and deep—it drew me close, and its impact continues to enrich my life each day. Thank You for guiding me in the ways of remaining steadfast in Your love.

To my beloved husband and best friend, Travis, and to my cherished Greene boys—Jace, Josh, and Judah: You embody God's unwavering love in my life. With profound gratitude I dedicate this book to each of you. Your presence has deepened my understanding of love and given me the gift of feeling truly cherished. Through your love, my connection with the Lord has thrived immeasurably.

Contents

Part 2: Discovering His Love   63

Remain in me, as I also remain in you. No branch can bear fruit by itself; it must remain in the vine. Neither can you bear fruit unless you remain in me.

JESUS

Introduction

For the past few years, I have been accepting, sharing, and living the message of permission. A life of permission happens when we flourish in the truth of who God says we are. And for as many times as I have shared this message, I continue to be amazed at how my permission to live free directly correlates with my acceptance of God's love for me. It is His consistent love as a father that fills the empty spaces and enhances the beautiful ones of my life. It is this love in which I want to remain and bear fruit. I desire the same for you.

Embracing our permission to live in His freedom and abundance comes in accepting who we are: God's beloved daughters. Our identity is confirmed. Our roles are established. The family dynamic is clear. We are heirs and joint heirs. We are considered beloved by God. We are loved. When we remain aware of and rooted in this godly identity, we are lavished in His love (1 John 3:1).

I invite you to join me in seeking a deeper intimacy between the Father and His daughter. Whether you have experienced a great relationship with your natural father or witnessed the devastation of an absent one, we're going to take hold of what it means to be loved by God. In the book of Romans, Paul writes, "For I am convinced that neither death nor life, neither angels nor demons, neither the present nor the future, nor any powers, neither height nor depth, nor anything else in all creation, will be able to separate us from the love of God that is in Christ Jesus our Lord" (Romans 9:38–39).

Sis, I am in full agreement: *nothing can separate us from the love of God*. So for the next 90 days, we'll dig deep into the riches of what it means to remain in the Father's love. Are you in?

To start, I want you to think about the names and attributes of God that you've heard. A few that always come to mind for me are:

Abba	Father
Jehovah Jireh	The Lord Our Provider
Jehovah Rapha	The Lord Our Healer
Jehovah Shammah	The Lord Is There
El Roi	The God Who Sees

And there are so many more! Notice how many names are characteristics that we often associate with fatherhood. Although we don't always receive these from our natural fathers, they are the steadfast, enduring qualities of God our Father, who does not fail.

I have divided this devotional into three parts for you: "Permission to Receive His Love," "Discovering His Love," and "Remaining in His Love." Being in a true, loving relationship with others requires vulnerability. Vulnerability requires self-awareness and self-love. And self-love requires a deep knowing of who you are—the good in you and the transformed parts of you. The three parts of this devotional will allow you to grow deeper in knowledge of yourself and God. After each 30-day collection, you will be invited to reflect on your experience. I ask you to thoughtfully respond before forging ahead. More importantly, I encourage you to use the exercises as a way to document your journey to remaining in love.

There is a refreshing freedom that comes with allowing God to be who He was designed to be in your life. Additionally, as His daughters we have access to abundance that others can't lay claim to. You deserve to live in the freedom and abundance that comes with being God's beloved daughter. Let's remain in His love together.

Love,

Dr. Jackie

Author's Note

CREATING SPACE

My freedom and your freedom come from being
fully and completely loved by God.
DR. JACKIE GREENE, *PERMISSION TO LIVE FREE*

Each time my husband and I prepared to welcome one of our boys into the world, there were certain things we did. We wanted to ensure that our home environment was ready for their arrival. They needed space for all their tiny baby things. We were excited to prepare the nursery space and lay out the best places for quick diaper changes in other parts of the house.

As the boys grew, we realized that we had to continue making adjustments to fit their presence in our home. Babyproofing was required for their early years of mobility—cover the outlets, move sharp objects, clear the roaming path. The routines and arrangement of our living areas have continued to evolve. I am reminded of the need to create space and make adjustments to support constant growth when I think of deepening my relationship with the Father. I begin each day by creating space to encounter Him. It's also the time when He brings necessary adjustments to my attention.

Quiet time and connecting with the Lord set our life in pace. When we stop and invite the Father in, we assume a position of humility. It is an acknowledgment that says, "God, I don't know what's going to happen on this day. I don't know how this is supposed to go." We have these things on our to-do lists, but we don't always know how to do them effectively without Him. So it's an admission of our need for Him. The pause for the moment of connection is a real reflection of our dependency and sets us up to find God's rhythm and flow for the day.

As we dig into these 90 days, I want to share more of what this practice of creating space looks like for me. You can use it as is or tweak it to fit your current life situation. It's a four-step exercise that starts my day with consistency. This devotional is actually a direct outcome of my daily practice.

Wait

I come into the space where I am quiet initially. Then I begin to pray in the Spirit. My praying in the Spirit is not always praying in tongues. Praying in the Spirit is praying according to the will of Holy Spirit. This means that I might be using words, but I'm being slow and considerate to what the Father wants to fill my mouth with. I wait instead of automatically rattling off my go-to prayers. During this time I have also learned to pause. I've learned to navigate, not being afraid of the silence. The goal of the wait is coming into agreement with what God wants to uniquely do in our time together that day. I'm waiting to sense His agenda and will for me and forsaking my own. I've found that His way is so much better for me!

Write

I follow my waiting time with writing. I always try to document where I am, even the days when I'm just not feeling it. I still choose to write in my journal and check in. I've never tried to bring God anything other than my honest, vulnerable self. I'm always focused on giving Him my truth so He can give me a greater truth. This practice makes space for Him to speak a better word over my words, so to speak.

In addition to writing about where I am, I thank God for the day. I tell Him how I feel about Him. I will write out the promises that I see in the Word that can be applicable to my life. Or if there is something that I read and I have a perspective on it, I write it down. Again, that's exactly how this devotional you're holding came to be. It was written in my journal before it was written to be shared with you.

While writing helps in the moment, it is also a wonderful way to track the ways He's moving and showing up for me. As a woman becoming anchored in the Lord, I keep my receipts by journaling! The enemy will come to lie and try to strip us of our faith. Being able to look back at the prayers God has answered and the words of affirmation He has spoken over me is necessary and effective. The receipts are reminders of all that God has done! This devo is filled with receipts.

Word

After waiting and using my writing to discern His will for the day, I engage with God's Word. Sometimes it is a devotional like this one. Other times it is my Bible. Even in my vulnerability I trust Him—through the Word of God, through the devotionals—to lead me to the books that will give me a better perspective. I want and need to be reminded of His promises. I go to whatever book I am studying and pull out the nuggets. "Oh, You promised Abraham that You are faithful? Then I know You will be faithful for Jackie."

Worship

The final portion of my clearing space is worship. I find a worship song that reflects how I'm feeling at the moment. Or I seek a song that reminds me of who I'm expecting God to be throughout my day. I offer it to Him as gratitude for the time we've spent together and the day He's set before me.

I invite you to try this framework as you go through the next three months:

Wait (make time)
Write (choose a journal)
Word (use this devotional)
Worship (create a playlist)

Make this practice yours. Being vulnerable in this way makes room for God's greater truth and love for us to manifest. Take note of the ways that your intimacy with the Father increases as a result of your intentional creation of space for Him at the beginning of your day.

Let's pray and get started.

Daddy, thank You for my sister holding this book in her hands. I pray that as we journey together, we discover new ways to experience Your love for us. Help us to walk out the next 90 days in the confidence of our identities as Your beloved daughters. Help us to not just start but stay consistent in building intimacy with You. Help us remain in Your love. In Jesus' name, amen.

PART 1

Permission to Receive His Love

*What identifies who we truly are is the fact
that we belong to God and are loved by Him.*
DR. JACKIE GREENE, *PERMISSION TO LIVE FREE*

In "Permission to Receive His Love," you are offered an invitation to learn or comprehend more deeply how wide and long and high and deep God's love is for you. The Lord desires that we come to own the beauty of this loving relationship with Him, regardless of our experiential frames of reference in our love with humans. God is love, and as you explore His nature in this section, I pray that the experience compels you to live freely in this love as God's beloved daughter. My sister, I pray that you find healing, new hope, and clarity on how very special you are as you navigate from page to page. God's love is refreshing, and once received, it has the power to reframe your whole world. I pray that you own and accept this love!

Close the Door

Think back to a relationship in which you wanted to spend as much time as you could with that individual. Before you met up with them, you would go through all the steps to ensure you were ready for the encounter. Hair. Nails. Outfit. Even if you weren't together in person yet, you found yourself preparing just in case you ran into them.

And let's not even get started on those early phone conversations! If you were like me as a teenager, you'd take the phone into your room, close the door, and settle in for a night of talking about absolutely nothing! Snacks. Music in the background. No interruptions. By the time you'd see them again in person, there was a familiarity resting between you. Knowing glances. Fluttering hearts. Satisfaction that you're in their physical presence again. It's almost like a breathtaking reward.

God desires that same type of intimacy with us. He wants us to go into our rooms, close the door, and talk to Him. Even though we can't see Him, we can hear Him and imagine His face as we pour out our hearts. We can imagine the smile stretching across His face when we share something that is pleasing to Him. And we can also envision the joy that radiates when He rewards us openly for something we discussed privately.

Start building intimacy with the Lord today through blocking off intentional time to communicate.

———

But when you pray, go into your room, close the door and pray to your Father, who is unseen. Then your Father, who sees what is done in secret, will reward you.

MATTHEW 6:6 (NIV)

——— *Prayer Prompt* ———

Abba, my desire is to know You intimately. Increase my desire to spend private time with You. Help me to close the doors of distraction . . .

The Place of Prayer

Have you ever been to a place so beautiful that you didn't want to leave? Or maybe you have pictures of these beautifully curated spaces on your Pinterest board. When I think of these settings, I think about restaurants, spas, and boutiques that I've visited. The attention to detail is so specific. There are often protocols in place to help you best enjoy the elaborate and lavish spreads to their fullest. The staff is poised to anticipate your needs. Your allergies have been noted by the kitchen. The sales consultant has pulled pieces she knows match your style. In settings like this, I don't want to rush in and out. Instead, I want to take my time and breathe in the full experience. I recognize these moments as valuable, precious, and often one of a kind. The place of prayer can also be like that for us.

Your time with God is so valuable and so precious. He knows what you need (Matt. 6:8). Like me when I'm shopping, I don't want you to rush the prayer experience with God. It's in the place of prayer that God is able to equip you for what's to come. He'll guide you in what to say and when to say it. He'll give you wisdom on what to do and when to do it. Remember that you have access to the Master of the universe! Return to the place of prayer!

Use your prayer time today to rediscover the grandeur of your place of prayer with the Father. Take in all that He has to offer during your time together—beautiful visions, clear instructions, perfect timing, and more.

———

Call to me and I will answer you and tell you great and unsearchable things you do not know.

JEREMIAH 33:3 (NIV)

Prayer Prompt

God, thank You for this time of prayer! Equip me and teach me how to do Your will . . .

God Sees You

Sis, you are wearing a lot of hats and doing a lot of things. You may be a faithful wife. Or perhaps you are a supportive sister and devoted daughter. At work you are going above and beyond to outperform your peers. And yet somehow you still feel invisible. I've been there before. So many times, we want the approval and affirmation of others. We want them to see us working hard, making progress, or doing something new. We want them to notice us.

I want to remind you today that even when people don't see you, God *always* does. The Father's eyes are always on you. As you are tempted to wallow in the discouragement of invisibility, I encourage you to keep going. Keep believing. Your efforts are not in vain. Neither are they going unnoticed. You are not invisible. God sees you!

I've heard children describe their parents as "having eyes in the back of their head" because it seems like their parents don't miss anything. God is like that. He embodies all the attributes of a good father, including seeing all things. He doesn't miss anything. Today I invite you to get to know the Father as **El Roi—the God who sees**. His eyes are always on you.

When it feels like others can't, don't, or simply won't, remember that God sees you.

Thereafter, Hagar used another name to refer to the LORD, who had spoken to her. She said, "You are the God who sees me."

GENESIS 16:13

Prayer Prompt

Lord, thank You for being El Roi. Thank You for seeing me! I will keep going knowing that my effort is not in vain . . .

Intimacy with God

When you hear the word "intimacy," what comes to mind? Something physical or tangible? A feeling or knowing? I think of intimacy as closeness and familiarity. As I look across standard examples and definitions, one thing is clear: *intimacy requires vulnerability.* Yet somehow the word "vulnerability" has gotten a bad rap. We've misidentified vulnerability with weakness and put things in place to avoid being seen as such. The result is us doing "all the right things" based on ritual or tradition. Though these are necessary things, they don't always allow us to really get to know the Lord. They are not a replacement for true intimacy with God.

When we come into relationship with a friend or spouse, we crave a certain level of connection. We desire to know as much as we can about the individual—their likes and dislikes. Similarly with business partners, we want to understand how they operate, what makes them move the needle of success. As new parents we take in everything about our children—counting their fingers and toes, breathing in their scent. All of these things point to intimacy. This is key in having a strong relational foundation. Likewise, intimacy is required for a strong relationship with the Lord.

Choose today to spend time learning true intimacy with Him. The intimate place is a safe place, one of power and true transformation. The intimate place is where you learn real love. The spiritual discipline of intimacy (seeking to know Him personally) should be our response to Him. A beautiful part of building intimacy with God is that there's no risk of Him not responding favorably.

When you share with Him, He will share with you. The intimacy is reciprocal, and this exchange of intimacy is love responding to love.

Come close to God, and God will come close to you.
JAMES 4:8

Prayer Prompt

Father, draw me close to You! I desire
to be fully vulnerable with You . . .

You Have to Decide

Intimacy is built through consistency. The more you spend time with an individual, the more intimacy is built—even with God. If we desire to grow in intimacy and knowledge, we have to continue to show up and engage with Him consistently.

I am often asked what helps to produce the most consistency in prayer, fasting, and reading the Word. The answer I always give is to *decide*! Before your flesh has time to disagree or your emotions have time to catch up, you have to make a firm decision about obeying God. Even when you don't feel like it, it's so important to not be ruled by what you feel and to do what you know is best for you.

Making a decision to engage in consistent intimacy with God means your actions will align! When the pandemic forced the world to pause in 2020, the Lord kept making clear to me that He wanted me to be up with Him every morning at five. When I finally made the decision to be consistent and honor that request, God met me. That time period is when my mentorship program, the Permission Room, was birthed. Everything came into alignment. It was as though He were just waiting for me to commit. That consistency has grown the Permission banner to serve thousands of women globally.

Spend time today reflecting on your consistency in building intimacy with the Father. I don't even want you to think back that far—just look at the past two weeks. Note the ways your consistency, or lack thereof, impacted your daily outcomes.

What decision do you need to make today to build more intimacy with the Lord?

But if serving the LORD seems undesirable to you, then choose for yourselves this day whom you will serve, whether the gods your ancestors served beyond the Euphrates, or the gods of the Amorites, in whose land you are living. But as for me and my household, we will serve the LORD.

JOSHUA 24:15 (NIV)

Prayer Prompt

Father, today I decide to follow You!
Empower me to make better decisions that
are in line with Your will for me . . .

He Decided

I was invited to a group chat with a woman working through a tough life decision. The problem was that the young woman had engaged in several conversations with other people before me. She'd already made up her mind on the decision she was facing. Me coming in wasn't going to change her perspective any more than the others who had tried. Any further conversation would have been futile. And I'm not one to argue with someone who has already stated their position. It's not fair to them or me. I promptly exited the conversation.

Years later I think about that moment when it comes to how we view ourselves versus how God sees us. Sometimes we've heard so many things about who we are, or what we're not, that our disposition is the same toward God. We've often already made up our minds about the kind of love we deserve. There are also moments when we've convinced ourselves that we're not worthy of any kind of love. Thankfully, God is patient with us when we're wrong. He doesn't leave us in the group chat of defeat. What He has decided about us supersedes anything we have decided about ourselves.

So can you stop fighting with God and agree with what He's already decided about you? Before time began God decided that you can be trusted with His resources. He's the one who gave you that leadership ability. He's the one who gave you that talent. He decided to make you different!

Stop saying you aren't good at it. Agree with God because He's already decided the truth about you.

Before I formed you in the womb I knew you,
  before you were born I set you apart;
  I appointed you as a prophet to the nations.
JEREMIAH 1:5 (NIV)

Prayer Prompt

Lord, I agree with what You've decided
about me! Show me the fullness of
who You've called me to be . . .

Your Yes Matters

Abraham and Sarah had every reason to say no when God promised them a child. Sarah straight up laughed in the faces of her husband and God. There was no way she was saying yes to having a child at her old age, especially since it hadn't happened in all of her and Abraham's history together. Then Abraham made the poor decision of agreeing with Sarah's plan to get with Hagar instead of waiting on God. Ishmael was born, but he wasn't the fulfillment of the promise. God's plan was so much larger than Abraham and Sarah could have expected or imagined. They wanted a son. God wanted generations. God wanted *nations*. It took Abraham and Sarah saying yes to God's specific plan for them. God needed a full *yes*. As a result of their *yes*, Isaac was born, leading to many generations. Their *yes* mattered so much that it impacts us today.

I want to remind you today that your *yes* is bigger than you! God wants to impact your children, your family, your legacy, your coworkers, and everyone connected to you. There is a ripple effect to our *yes*! God will honor your push and your sacrifice. He is faithful to bring generational blessings through our obedience!

Your yes is not in vain: your children's children will be impacted by the decisions you make today. For the aunties reading this, your nieces, nephews, and godchildren will also be beneficiaries.

I will confirm my covenant with you and your descendants after you, from generation to generation. This is the everlasting covenant: I will always be your God and the God of your descendants after you.

GENESIS 17:7–8

Prayer Prompt

Father, I will continue to give You my yes!
Thank You for Your faithfulness to my
bloodline and those connected to me . . .

The Real You

In my book *Permission to Live Free*, I shared a story about how a grade school incident involving chemical hair straighteners led to me constantly wearing extensions. Years later I realized that I'd come to rely on those hair weaves as a convenient cover-up for feelings of inadequacy. I was not living as my true self, the real masterpiece God had created me to be. It would take years to fully accept the permission God gave me to be the real me. I had to make the choice to see who God sees. To not give in to what I feel but to instead live in the truth. Now I often remind myself of who I really am—God's masterpiece.

Did you know that you, too, have been created as a masterpiece by God? That means you don't have to fabricate or create a new version of yourself. God created you with the good things that He's planned for you already in mind. So everything you need—skill sets, gifts, and talents—are already present in your life because He knew what He was fashioning you for.

Settle today that you will no longer dim your true light to fit in because you think that's what the world wants. Consider releasing things that you have been utilizing as fillers to absorb the impact of inadequate feelings.

The best gift you can give anyone is the real you! This is where our true power resides.

For we are God's masterpiece. He has created us anew in Christ Jesus, so we can do the good things he planned for us long ago.

EPHESIANS 2:10

Prayer Prompt

Daddy, this day I choose to live as the masterpiece You created me to be . . .

Be a Daughter

Out of all the titles you may have—mother, wife, entrepreneur, pastor, teacher—the most important title you'll ever wear is that of daughter. And based on our unique lives, that title holds different weight for each of us. You may have lived under the shame of being an unknown daughter. Or perhaps you basked in the spoiled protection of being the only daughter in a family full of boys. In both scenarios the fact remains that you are a daughter.

We're all daughters of the King with the permission to reign. This permission comes without the need to perform. Performing is for clowns anyway. You don't have to perform for God! All you have to do is receive Him as **Abba Father.**

Research has shown that the father-daughter relationship holds immense significance. And not just through the early years—it matters throughout every phase of development including our adulthood. Whether with our biological father, or someone else in that role, we benefit from being seen, cared for, and loved as daughters. There is a wholeness that comes when our position as a daughter is acknowledged and those needs are met. Studies have reported that young women who experience healthy relationships with their fathers are less likely to become clinically depressed or anxious.[1] Additional benefits include increased confidence, enhanced communication skills, balanced perspectives, and emotional security. If these are the natural results, imagine the outcomes of being in healthy relationships with Abba!

Today I encourage you to accept your permission to walk like a daughter of the Most High King. What does that look like for you? Maybe your head is held a little higher. Maybe you stand a bit taller. Or better yet, maybe your stride is a little surer.

Whatever that permission looks like for you, walk in it, sis. Be the daughter that you are.

"I will be a Father to you, and you will be my sons and daughters, says the Lord Almighty."

2 CORINTHIANS 6:18 (NIV)

Prayer Prompt

Lord, thank You for making me Your daughter!
Teach me how to reign with You . . .

Feed Your Decision

There's a popular phrase that says, "You are what you eat." I often think about this when it comes to our decision to follow Christ. Like human relationships, remaining in love with God takes work. Each day requires a decision to feed the relationship what it needs to grow and bear fruit. Our decisions to build intimacy with God through consistency and to agree with what He's decided about us require nourishment. For me, this looks like reading books and devotionals that reinforce what I have decided. I listen to songs that remind me of the decision and its benefits. I am attracted to words and refrains that remind me of who God is in our relationship. I cling to the promises He's made to me. I immerse myself in the choice.

Once you have decided to follow Jesus, you must feed the decision you've made! Put yourself in environments that support your decision to follow Christ. Go to church, get in community, stay in the Word, and pray continuously. Spend intentional time with God. Feeding yourself with these spiritual disciplines will keep you going in the direction of following God! Eventually the fruit you bear will look like what you have been feeding yourself.

Make a plan for feeding your decision to be in relationship with God. Identify one habit to incorporate into your daily spiritual routine to feed your decision.

I am the vine; you are the branches. If you remain in me and I in you, you will bear much fruit; apart from me you can do nothing.

JOHN 15:5 (NIV)

Prayer Prompt

Lord, I have decided to follow You! Help me to feed the decision I've made so that I may grow closer to You . . .

You Matter

Hey sis, I don't know if you've heard this lately, but *you matter*. Just as you are. I've had to remind myself of this truth more than I'd like to admit. We matter. Apart from our titles. Separate from our roles and responsibilities. Say it with me: "I matter." Now say it with your chest, like you mean it: "I MATTER!"

Something shifts when you accept the truth that God hand-crafted and uniquely designed you. With the media and society pushing us to abandon our diversity in favor of assimilation, we must hold fast to the truth that our existence holds significance. The moment you or I conform to the way of the world, we leave a void for the thing we were created to do.

The world needs you to be who you're called to be. There is no one like *you*. Your life matters! In fact, God calls you His own special treasure. We've been set apart as holy and chosen. No matter what your past experiences are, you're still a valuable, special treasure set aside for His will and good pleasure. You have permission to walk fully into who you're called to be because we need the skills, gifts, and talents that God has placed in you.

As you go throughout the day, I encourage you to take note of your uniqueness. When the voice of doubt attempts to creep up, stop it with a firm reminder: "I matter!"

You have been set apart as holy to the LORD your God, and he has chosen you from all the nations of the earth to be his own special treasure.

DEUTERONOMY 14:2

Prayer Prompt

Thank You, Lord, for designing me precisely.
Help me to bring to life everything that
You've placed on the inside of me . . .

God Made

When we hold newborn babies, our hearts swell with how perfect they are. We inhale their smells and take in all their features. It's amazing how much detail is put into such a tiny creature. If they're your own child or the child of someone close to you, it's not uncommon to get caught up in examining everything about them. We watch them sleep, in awe of how they're made. We consider what the future may hold for them. Who will they become? What will they accomplish? Tiny babies are captivatingly good for so many reasons. Likewise, when God created you, He immediately decided that you were good. In great anticipation He created you in His image with specific purposes in mind. And to this very day He is still taking in your goodness with expectation for who and how He made you.

We were *all* born on purpose, for a purpose: to fulfill a God-given assignment here on earth. But the only way we fully do this is by returning to the way we were originally created. Not self-made but *God*-made. We're not trying to have life outside of God, but we want to live our lives in continual communion with Him. This is where He continues to remind us of His desire, and we're able to carry out our assignment the way He designed us to. Remaining in His love for us is the key to carrying out our unique assignments.

Spend some time today examining the places in your life and your heart that may be more self-made than God-made. How can you return to your God-made, God-breathed, purpose-filled settings?

God saw all that he had made, and it was very good. And there was evening, and there was morning—the sixth day.

GENESIS 1:31 (NIV)

Prayer Prompt

Lord, thank You for creating me on purpose.
Infuse me with Your breath so that I will
carry out my assignment Your way . . .

For a Reason

I've heard stories about and witnessed friends using work-arounds to solve problems. I've been guilty of doing the same. One instance that comes to mind is when I began to use motherhood, a true gift, as my security blanket. It helped soothe my insecurities and fears associated with this new and unknown life, which was at the time my present reality. Unfortunately, I found myself misusing what was supposed to be a temporary fix as a long-term solution. I was hiding and avoiding other responsibilities and opportunities. What I thought I would use only temporarily became the stronghold that led to me losing my voice, my courage, and my ability to take any new steps.

Motherhood was new and different, but it's still a gift that God desired so desperately to use. It gave me a nurturing outlook and taught me service to others in a different way. My paralysis was nurtured by the security blanket of motherhood. It felt safer than daring to find out the true use for this new gift. I've seen this happen to others. We use gifts to meet the need of a moment, and over time we notice they're not as potent because of our misuse.

That pattern stops today. God is not a God who wastes anything. Even if it's been misused, regardless if it's been abused, and especially if it's been overlooked. God's gifting in you exists for a reason. Don't allow the enemy to talk you out of using what

God gave you (the gift of faith, of loving people, of being generous, etc.). *Use them!*

Ask Holy Spirit to reveal gifts you may have discounted. Note what is shared and meditate on God's Word concerning those gifts. Expect a response for how to use them for His glory.

We have different gifts, according to the grace given to each of us. If your gift is prophesying, then prophesy in accordance with your faith; if it is serving, then serve; if it is teaching, then teach; if it is to encourage, then give encouragement; if it is giving, then give generously; if it is to lead, do it diligently; if it is to show mercy, do it cheerfully.

ROMANS 12:6–8 (NIV)

Prayer Prompt

God, thank You for these gifts You've given me! Show me how to use them according to Your will . . .

Heart, Soul, Mind, and Strength

When it comes to love and relationships, I've heard people describe how their heart is telling them one thing, but their head is telling them another. This disconnect makes it hard to make decisions. However, when our hearts and minds are in alignment, moving forward is possible. Especially when it comes to love.

That's what was happening to Sandra in her early dating life. Her heart, and outsiders, kept telling her that it was time to get married and that a particular guy would fit the bill. Her heart had her believing that he was to be her husband. In her heart Sandra loved him as a person, but her mind recognized something was off. As a result, her soul and strength were being put to the test.

She was praying for clarity. She was using all her strength and effort to make the relationship work. It was a back-and-forth between her personal desire to be married now and sensing God's guidance to wait. Eventually she yielded: this wasn't the guy she was going to marry. When Sandra did finally meet the one, she couldn't believe the peace that came. She was captivated by how God's love for her was tangible through this new relationship. Her heart, soul, mind, and strength were in alignment with God and her new boo. No more tug-of-war.

Our greatest commandment is not just to love God, but to do it with all our heart, soul, mind, and strength. As I was praying about this passage, the Lord impressed on my heart to not leave any space in me that is not fully saturated with love for Him! This closes the door for anything else to be lord in any area of your life. God must be Lord in our hearts, our minds, and our souls. Pour your love on your Father today!

What area of your life needs to be saturated in God's love to move forward?

Love the Lord your God with all your heart and with all your soul and with all your mind and with all your strength.

MARK 12:30 (NIV)

Prayer Prompt

Lord, I love You! Teach me how to make
You Lord of every area of my life . . .

You've Got the Power

There's an early '90s song by Snap! that is often played at basketball games and other live events. The song is so recognizable that on hearing the first notes, long before lyrics cover the funky bass line, audiences automatically get ready to move and enjoy the excitement. Many of them feel compelled to belt out the lyrics. The song has been out for decades, yet its hype has not died down. There is something about acknowledging "I've got the power" that gives energy to whatever is coming next. I feel the same way when it comes to Christ. His presence in my heart is a reminder that I've got the power!

Sis, do you realize how much power is in you? You have power because Christ, the Hope of Glory, is inside you! The power that works within you has never been intimidated. The Spirit of God shows up strong in your godly DNA. Be assured, confident, and bold, knowing that what's within you is not passive, but powerful!

Today is a wonderful day to walk in the confidence of Christ's power. If you are facing a challenge, walk with the assurance of sharing His glory.

For God wanted them to know that the riches and glory of Christ are for you Gentiles, too. And this is the secret: Christ lives in you. This gives you assurance of sharing his glory.

COLOSSIANS 1:27

Prayer Prompt

Lord, I thank You that the same power that is in You is also in me. I will walk in the power You've given me . . .

Remember What God Said

"But what did I say?" I overheard the coach speaking to his player. The teenager was attempting to justify another play a parent on the sidelines was suggesting. At that moment I was reminded of how often God has said one thing, but we hear and value the voices of others more. Social media influencers and online trends have convinced us: *You should do it this way. You aren't good enough the way you are. The only way that will work is if. . .* We try to justify why we haven't done what God called us to do: *My platform isn't as big as hers. I don't look like all the other people out there doing it. Based on my past, no one is going to listen to me.* But what has God said?

Today I'm challenging you to *believe* what your Creator has said about you. Everyone else will always have something to say, but what our Father says matters most! Let's have the audacity to believe what *He* said! When we remember His voice alone, we become unstoppable.

When was the last time that you reminded yourself of what God has said concerning you? Take time to write down what He's said to and about you.

How precious are your thoughts about me, O God. They cannot be numbered! I can't even count them; they out-number the grains of sand! And when I wake up, you are still with me!

PSALM 139:17–18

Prayer Prompt

Lord, I will remember what You have said about me. When other voices come, help me to remind myself of Your word concerning me . . .

Freedom Is Available

For more than a decade Mother Shirley utilized the assistance of canes and walkers. She even learned to enjoy her grandchildren riding on the mobile scooters with her through the grocery store. Mother Shirley was fairly comfortable with the work-arounds of her condition until a doctor's visit challenged her comfort level. "Do you want more freedom to move around on your own?" The doctor recommended hip replacement surgery to increase her mobility. However, the catch to enjoying this mobility was how hard Mother Shirley was willing to work in the rehabilitation phase of her healing journey. The doctor could replace the ailing hip, but she would have to do the exercises necessary to enjoy the newfound freedom. She'd spend months with the physical therapy team relearning the old skill of walking. There would be days when she didn't feel like going for follow-up medical visits. Certainly days would come when the therapists tested her physical limits. Was it worth it?

Mother Shirley thought of the things she had missed because of her fear of falling. She recalled the effects of her body's deterioration and the emotional pain that accompanied each change. Then she envisioned what it would be like to be fully present and engaged with her grandchildren without the cumbersome canes and walkers. The doctor was offering her freedom, and she took it.

God is fully aware of our past experiences, and He is clear about our current condition. This should provide us with reassurance, hope, and courage that we don't have to stay in our current condition. Our Father knows exactly what we're facing, and He has a plan to redeem us! Don't forget—we don't have to stay bound. There is freedom available!

Spend time today thinking about the areas in which you've been bound. Do you want to be healed? Remember freedom is available.

When Jesus saw him lying there and knew that he had already been there a long time, he said to him, "Do you want to be healed?"

JOHN 5:6 (ESV)

Prayer Prompt

Thank You, Lord, for knowing every detail of my life! I choose to walk in the freedom that's available to me . . .

No Reason to Fear

Science teaches us that the body has a few response choices to fear: fight, flight, or freeze. Fear looks different on everyone—it's not always the scared emoji in our phones. When backed in a corner by danger, you may be inclined to come out swinging. Straight-up ready to fight. The second response is to go into flight mode, abandoning the situation. Running faster than Forrest Gump in the other direction. The last fear response is freezing. Staying stuck right where you are, waiting for whatever is going to happen.

Can you identify with any of these responses? They're all natural; however, I am reminded that our spirits have a different option. The Word tells us that God has not given us the spirit of fear but of power, love, and a sound mind (2 Tim. 1:7). Through Christ we have the option to respond with power and courage. We can stand boldly and extend love in the direction of our opposition. Having a sound mind allows us to stand firm in God's Word and promises.

But Dr. Jackie, what's the difference between standing firm and standing still? Freezing, or standing still, immobilizes you. There is no progress or change when you are frozen in fear. Standing firm is about choosing to stick with Jesus no matter what fear is attempting to deliver to your feet.

As fear tries to make its way into your life, stand firm and see the salvation of the Lord! Irrespective of what may be in front of you or what may be surrounding you, God is faithful to protect you, cover you, and provide for you! You don't have any reason to fear. Whatever you're facing, you can believe that God is in the middle of it. Watch Him turn it around!

What are you currently facing today that tempts you to respond in fight, flight, or freeze mode? How can you exchange that posture for power, love, and a sound mind?

And Moses said to the people, "Fear not, stand firm, and see the salvation of the LORD, which he will work for you today. For the Egyptians whom you see today, you shall never see again."

EXODUS 14:13 (ESV)

Prayer Prompt

Lord, thank You that I have no reason to fear. Teach me how to stand firm instead of freezing, fleeing, or fighting . . .

Can You See?

Have you ever played one of those games where you are shown a small portion of an image? The goal is to guess what the image is before your opponent does or before the timer goes off and the entire picture is revealed. When playing with a group, the game gets loud and rowdy as people shout out their answers. Some players seem inclined to guess scary or negative things. Then there are those who have outlandish "there's no way an answer that unrelated would ever end up in this game" predictions. And then there are individuals who have an uncanny sense of imagery and can make an accurate guess from any thumbnail-sized photo. This game is like a mix of Pictionary and inkblot tests—name what you think you see. In all three activities the responses to pictures can tell a lot about a person.

God has a picture for our lives. He's **Alpha and Omega— the Beginning and the End**, so He already knows what the full picture contains. The challenge is for us to see the full picture too. Unfortunately, life has a way of weathering down our perspective. Over time we find ourselves looking for the negative. We focus on what's missing or imperfect, which leads to a limited view of God's truth. And the enemy can't see the full picture either, but he knows that it's something magnificent. He begins shouting out the untruths and causing us to get distracted. The enemy will do all he can to limit your ability to see the goodness that God has given you in your life. Limited sight leads to limited expectations, limited money, and limited choices. I believe God desires to remove our limitations by healing us to recognize what we have. He's been so good to us—don't let the enemy rob you of your ability to see!

Set a five-minute timer and write down all the goodness of God you can see in your life right now. Refer to this list often.

Now we see things imperfectly, like puzzling reflections in a mirror, but then we will see everything with perfect clarity. All that I know now is partial and incomplete, but then I will know everything completely, just as God now knows me completely.

1 CORINTHIANS 13:12

Prayer Prompt

Lord, I'm grateful that You gave me the ability to see. Show me the goodness in everything You've given me . . .

You Have Authority

When Jody was younger, her mother sometimes left her with her older and younger brothers for the day while she went to work during the summer. Jody was often put in charge because of her sense of responsibility. She delivered firm instructions with her hands on her hips and a stern face, mimicking her mother. While Jody was often teased for how she presented her newfound authority, she never wavered because she knew how important it was for things to go smoothly while her mom was out of the house. She didn't lord her authority over her brothers. She didn't try to overstate her authority or use it in other situations. Jody simply took her job seriously.

Like Jody, you have been given specific instructions. You have authority on earth to be and do what God has called you to. Understanding and accepting His authority in you is a posture that you should always walk in. You are a child of the Most High King! You have authority in Christ. Be encouraged and continue to walk in the authority given to you by the Lord.

Take inventory today of how you are walking into rooms and situations. In what ways are you walking with boldness and authority? Which situations cause you to shrink back?

Look, I have given you authority over all the power of the enemy, and you can walk among snakes and scorpions and crush them. Nothing will injure you.

LUKE 10:19

Prayer Prompt

Lord, as I go throughout my day, I will remember to walk in Your authority. Show me how to live out my authority in You . . .

Nothing Wasted

Ethan Hunt, the character played by Tom Cruise in the *Mission Impossible* movies, is a resourceful secret agent. No matter what situation he's faced with, Hunt always finds a way out. One of the things that I love about these movies is that Hunt is able to look around his setting and use whatever he can get his hands on as a part of the solution to the problem he is facing. He rarely overlooks the small things and always finds a way to use everything within reach to his advantage. His innovation and adaptation mean that nothing goes unused. Nothing is wasted.

I have found myself in situations when I didn't know how I was going to get to the other side. And I certainly didn't think that those encounters would be of any use once I got out of them. Thankfully God's ways are not my ways. He's a resourceful father able to weave crushing moments into victories and testimonies time and time again. He's used it all—the good, the bad, and the ugly—to His glory. Nothing is wasted.

God is able to mold every decision you make for His glory. Some of our worst mistakes become our biggest blessings. That means even your *worst* mistake is usable. Don't try to control your own story. Hand everything back to the one who wrote your story, and let Him show you the good that He's able to bring out of it all!

What experience, decision, or mistake have you discarded? Ask God to reveal its connection to His glory in your life.

When they had all had enough to eat, he said to his disciples, "Gather the pieces that are left over. Let nothing be wasted."

JOHN 6:12 (NIV)

Prayer Prompt

Lord, I thank You for using every part of my story . . .

You Had to Go Through

When I was a teenager, I had a terrible accident in my brand-new car after dozing off at the wheel. I woke to find myself tumbling down a steep embankment and flipping through the air. My phone was lost, and I had to walk miles to get to help. By the grace of God, I lived to tell the story to you today. Though my car was totaled, I walked away with only a small scratch on my leg.

The lasting lesson would come months later through a conversation with my mom. I had to go through that difficult experience to see myself differently. You see, the circumstances surrounding that accident were layered and complicated. I'd snuck a guy over to visit. We had a fight. I totaled my car. I lied to my mom. And I was ashamed about it all. It took me hitting rock-bottom to learn more about who I was—especially under pressure. It would take time to learn how to stand in my truth.

Your experience may not be as dramatic as mine, or maybe it was even harder, but I'm sure you've had a tough time or two. It's in these moments that the Lord will allow your life to pass through a specific circumstance, location, or crisis. Though often uncomfortable, these are necessary for God to set up a divine encounter—right in the middle of that circumstance—to draw you near to Him. Pay close attention to the places God allows you to pass through. He has intention in every single step! You had to go through it . . . through there . . . through that . . . to find your way to the place you would meet or reconnect with the Lord. Don't try to avoid an encounter that your life can't afford to live without!

What lessons in recent going-through-it moments stand out as God getting your attention? How can you use those encounters in your next phase of life?

So he left Judea and went back once more to Galilee. Now he had to go through Samaria.

JOHN 4:3-4 (NIV)

Prayer Prompt

Lord, thank You for ordering my steps. Show me why You had to take me that way . . .

45

It's Not Over

A little girl I know loves this family spy show on television. On a few episodes the action has gotten really intense, and just as the heroes get stuck in an impossible situation, "to be continued" flashes across the screen and the credits roll. She always responds in disbelief at how the show could end an episode with a cliff-hanger. We already know the hero is going to be okay—otherwise there would be no show at all. Yet we still have to remind this little girl that it's just the end of the episode—another one is coming. She just has to be patient. If the show is on a streaming service, the next episode is coming right away. There's even an option to skip the "previously on . . ." recap and get right to the action. If it's a weekly show on a network, another episode will air next week and pick up right where the scene left off. We also chuckle a little bit as we remind her that she has these options. Not that long ago television was live only—meaning we really had to wait to see what happens next. And if we missed it, we missed it!

How many times in our own lives do we respond like this little girl? We get nervous about what's to come in a seemingly impossible situation. We start to panic and desire to know the outcome right away. We want to skip the replays of what we've already been through and get to the good part. After all, we already know how our story is going to end—victoriously.

Whenever you face unfavorable situations, be reminded that God can use them for His glory! He works everything for your good. Whatever situation you might find yourself in, it's not over until it's good! If it's not good, it must not be the end. Encourage yourself today: *it's not over*!

Ask the Lord to help you see Him in the circumstance.

And we know that God causes everything to work together for the good of those who love God and are called according to his purpose for them.

ROMANS 8:28

Prayer Prompt

Lord, it's not over until You say it's over! Teach me how to stay focused on Your goodness . . .

Prayer Is a Tool

Angela was putting together a bookshelf for her home office. She'd ordered this particular shelf because of how easy the reviews said it was to assemble. It was one of those designs that required only a hammer; the other necessary tools were provided. As she began to assemble the shelf, Angela found herself struggling with the screws. *Looks like I need a screwdriver too.* As she paused to evaluate the situation, she realized two things: (1) The screws didn't have grooves for a screwdriver, and (2) she was using the provided Allen wrench all wrong. At that moment Angela realized that tools are only as good as their proper usage. When she started to use the wrench correctly, her time was cut in half and her frustration dissipated. She finished the bookshelf and put it in a corner of her office.

Like Angela, we each have a specific assignment to carry out here on earth. The Bible says that God has given us all we need for life and godliness. There are a lot of things that I've gained in life that have helped me become the person I am, but I would have to say *nothing* has consistently changed me from season to season more than prayer. Once I learned how to effectively use prayer as a tool, I was able to execute more of what the Father was calling me to.

If you are frustrated and feel that you aren't growing, you have to up your prayer life. I want you to know it's a tool that truly works! Prayer has lifted me in moments when I felt I had nothing left to give. It's shifted my perspective and forced me to see with new eyes. Prayer has eased many frustrations and become my lifeline!

Prayer is most effective when it's used for everything. Challenge yourself to pray throughout the day about everything, including the seemingly small things. Note how you feel at the end of the day.

Don't worry about anything; instead, pray about everything. Tell God what you need, and thank him for all he has done.

PHILIPPIANS 4:6

Prayer Prompt

Today I commit to prayer! Take me to
new levels of prayer, Lord . . .

It Has to Go

"Bag Lady" is a popular song by artist Erykah Badu. The lyrics urge the woman to put down all the bags she's collected over the course of her lifetime. Each time I hear the song, I'm reminded of Hebrews 12:1, which admonishes us to lay aside every weight and every sin to run our race. While it's easy to name the sin, the weight is another story. We don't always recognize the weight we're carrying because we've been lugging it around for so long. Yes, our arms and backs grow stronger. But our pace is slower. Our endurance gives out.

If we want to be strong contenders in the race of life and faith, the extra baggage has to go. Hurt? Has to go. Disappointment? Can't stay. Shame? Not ours to carry. Abandonment and rejection issues? Take them out of the bag. Negative words spoken over us? Drop them off. Unproductive habits? Cut them out. Inconsistency? Uproot it. Whatever your "it" is, *it has to go.*

There are so many things we've picked up along life's journey that have to go. We must not be convinced or persuaded to believe words that are not from the mouth of our Father. Any word in opposition to God's Word is a lie! We must expel the actions, beliefs, and behavior patterns that are in opposition to God's promises. They must be uprooted so they don't continue to grow in new seasons. So the weeds don't continue to choke out the harvests. That means if something didn't come from Him, *it has to go*! The God of truth is always with you! Only believe the words of your Abba. You have permission to uproot it all and let it go.

Do not settle for a lie when the truth is present.

Jesus replied, "Every plant not planted by my heavenly Father will be uprooted."

MATTHEW 15:13

Prayer Prompt

Lord, I want Your truth alone! Uproot
the lies of the enemy . . .

Yesterday Is Not Today

If I had one dollar for every time I've heard someone resist trying something again because it previously failed, I'd be a multi-millionaire. But I've been there too. I've had high hopes for certain outcomes in my life that didn't go as planned. I've given my all to things with grand expectations. And it simply didn't work out. Maybe it was the wrong timing. Maybe it was the wrong connection. Maybe it was the wrong location.

Whatever the "it" was doesn't change the level of disappointment we experience. I've had moments where I just wanted to give up. And let's not get into my frustration when I saw the very thing that hadn't worked out for me working for other people. I had to swap my frustrated view for a faith view. My faith reminded me that God "is the same yesterday, today, and forever" (Heb. 13:8). It says so right in His Word. His reliability and trustworthiness would be the same for me. I just needed to be patient and allow Him to work on my behalf in His timing. Once I surrendered to His will and His way, He absolutely blew my mind. He breathed on what I was trying to make live through my own efforts. The life that He brought to my situation was so new, so fresh, that I couldn't have made up a better storyline. If I'd allowed my disappointment to win over, I would have missed out. I had to be willing and humble enough to try again.

Listen to me, beloved sister: yesterday is not today. It may not have gone how you wanted it to last time, but the disappointment of yesterday is the God-ordained setup of today! God is doing a *new* thing. Circumstances may look and feel the same, but with God everything has the ability to change. It's a new day, so that means there's a new opportunity for God to bring about a new outcome. In our disappointment He's God, and in our triumph He's God.

Take a moment today to name your disappointments over past failures. Which ones do you need to trust God to make new?

Simon answered, "Master, we've worked hard all night and haven't caught anything. But because you say so, I will let down the nets."

LUKE 5:5 (NIV)

Prayer Prompt

Daddy, thank You for a new day! At Your word, I will try again . . .

Come Back

A 2023 global news story highlighted an Indian father, Prem Gupta, welcoming his daughter home. The story was captivating because the daughter's marriage had ended badly, usually an occurrence considered a blemish on the woman and her family in their culture. Yet it was the father's response that spoke volumes—loud enough to drown out the whispers of disgrace. He organized a baraat to welcome her back. Traditionally a baraat is a celebratory processional for the groom heading to the bride's home for their wedding. This father's choice was unconventional and went against societal norms, all for his beloved daughter. He was sending a clear message regarding his love and support for her. With great fanfare the daughter's return was reminiscent of the story of the prodigal son in Luke 15. Sakshi Gupta returned to her father's arms with fireworks, music, and celebration.[2]

I am aware of how hard it can be to get back up and return to our places of safety when the unexpected in life has knocked us down. I pray in this moment that if you are in a fallen or wounded state, you will hear the song of the Lord wooing you to get back up and come to Him.

No matter your situation—bad, toxic, embarrassing, disappointing—the Father's love can cover it. The Father wants you to come back to Him just as you are! Don't try to fix yourself up outside of His presence. He ultimately knows what's best and how to get you back to the God-created version of you that He created in the beginning. Surrender it all to allow the Father to do all that He desires! He's calling you back to Him with open arms.

Which areas in your life have you been trying to get together on your own before coming back to the Father? Recognize today that He welcomes you back just as you are.

However, those the Father has given me will come to me, and I will never reject them.

JOHN 6:37

Prayer Prompt

God, today I run back to Your open arms. Thank You for loving me . . .

The Mindset of Freedom

I came across a 1949 interview of Mr. Fountain Hughes, a formerly enslaved man, through the Folklife Today podcast series *Voices from the Days of Slavery: Stories, Songs and Memories*. A particular memory Hughes shared about life after freedom stood out to me:

> We was just turned out like a lot of cattle. You know how they turn cattle out in a pasture? Well, after freedom, you know, colored people didn't have nothing. Colored people didn't have no beds when they was slaves. We always slept on the floor, pallet here, and a pallet there just like . . . a lot of . . . wild people . . . we didn't . . . we didn't know nothing. [The slave owners] didn't allow you to look at no book.[3]

His family's life in freedom still had its challenges. They still slept wherever. They still survived with little to no resources. Undoubtedly, after generations enslaved, it would take time to undo the thinking and patterns of behavior while building a new future. Yet they persevered.

Imagine if Mr. Hughes and his family had decided that living free was just as hard as living enslaved. They could have returned to plantations for bond work and would have settled for the life they knew. I think about the Israelites complaining in

Exodus 14. They wondered if returning to Pharaoh's rule would have been better than the journey to freedom in the wilderness. Nothing good would have come out of that choice.

God is fully aware of how our years of bondage can linger with us even in freedom. He reminds us in Galatians 5:1 to stand firm and not be burdened again by a yoke of slavery. Our yokes of slavery are our past experiences and the mindsets that hold us there. The yoke represents the attitudes that tie us to the old place, preventing us from living in the abundance of the free place. The freedom mindset offers us reassurance, hope, and courage. Your Father knows exactly what you're facing and still has a plan to redeem you!

Don't forget: once you're free, your attitude must shift to sustain your liberty in the new place.

. . . to be made new in the attitude of your minds.
EPHESIANS 4:23 (NIV)

Prayer Prompt

Thank You, Lord, for bringing me to a
place of freedom. Help me develop a new
attitude and mindset to match . . .

Nothing Is Impossible

When our oldest son was learning long division, he became frustrated. It seemed the more we tried to help him, the less progress was being made. After one particularly difficult attempt, he declared the learning impossible. He didn't want our help. And he didn't want to spend any more time on that skill. In his young mind, he could live without it—especially if it was going to be that hard.

I felt the same way when I was in dental school learning how to cut my first crown prep. Everything about this one procedure seemed impossible, and I wanted to give up. Now when I reflect on that part of the journey and my son's experience, I have to chuckle at how monumental both challenges felt. We both needed support outside ourselves. When we admitted our shortcomings and accepted help, the impossible became possible.

Sometimes we call things impossible when really, they are just hard, inconvenient, or simply new to us. An African proverb I heard says, "One who says it cannot be done shouldn't stand in the way of the person doing it." Listen, it may be hard for you, but it's not hard for God. Get out of the way so that He can do the impossible! What is that thing that you've looked at and already decided that it's too hard for God? Trust me, He is *more than able* to deliver on His Word! Nothing is impossible for Him.

Ask yourself what things you've written off as impossible. Invite the Father into your situation.

Jesus looked at them and said, "With man this is impossible, but with God all things are possible."

MATTHEW 19:26 (NIV)

Prayer Prompt

Lord, reveal Yourself to me! Step into my hard situations and show me that nothing is impossible . . .

Sorry, Not Sorry

When she was a little girl, Brittany saw a boy step on a caterpillar. All of the guts and goo puddled around the fuzzy exterior. She began to avoid caterpillars squirming on the pavement because they made her skin feel like it was crawling. Now she understands the life cycle of insects, but she still avoids stepping on them. Brittany wants them to reach their full potential as beautiful butterflies with the purpose of pollinating plants. Their work helps plants, fruits, and vegetables produce new seeds.

Did you catch that? The majority of plants need butterflies (and bees) to help them reproduce! And more often than not, when we see a butterfly, we rarely think of what its life was like when it was just a velvety caterpillar. We don't try to envision butterflies struggling in a cocoon. Instead, we admire the beauty and grace with which they flutter around. It's interesting how we as people can extend this grace to small insects but struggle to find this same appreciation for others. We struggle to see people for who they are now as opposed to who they were in past struggles.

Once a person has lived a particular lifestyle for so long, it's difficult for others to see them as anything else—especially if they've been around for a long time. I won't even get started on how people treat us when we're in the cocoon phase of our lives, struggling to emerge as something more. It's hard. But when we break out, there's a tremendous beauty and glory that makes us want to flutter in full freedom. Unfortunately, not everyone's ready to encounter us that way.

Have you ever revisited a space God has delivered you from with old friends who haven't witnessed your transition? Did you try to be your old self to fit in again? Or were you just uncomfortable the whole time? It is in those moments that God allows you to see all the work that He has done in your life. He has made you *new*, so walk in it! Don't apologize for it—sorry, not sorry! We're gonna be what God said.

Who has God called you to be unapologetically in this season?

Obviously, I'm not trying to win the approval of people, but of God. If pleasing people were my goal, I would not be Christ's servant.

GALATIANS 1:10

Prayer Prompt

Lord, I will make no apologies for being who You've called me to be. Teach me how to humbly and boldly walk in my new identity . . .

Permission to Receive His Love

Accepting permission to be loved doesn't look the same for everyone. Some of us have known we were loved since the day we were born, while others have had to go through a few things before we could consider that we might be worthy of being loved. No matter where you are on the spectrum, be honest about your current place of really feeling and experiencing love. Do you just know it in your head, or do you experience it in your life? Before you begin the next 30 days, take a moment to think about how you do or do not experience being loved. As you think about permission to be loved, notice the areas where it is a bit more challenging to accept God's love in your deep places. Also note the places where you feel the most confidence.

- When I think about being loved . . .
- Ways that I know I am loved by family and friends . . .
- Ways that I know I am loved by God . . .
- I feel most loved when . . .

PART 2

Discovering His Love

*Human love isn't perfect love. It can
be really special, but ultimately there
is only one love that never fails.*
DR. JACKIE GREENE, *PERMISSION TO LIVE FREE*

When we're children, we don't always understand why our parents and caregivers do what they do. When we become adults ourselves, we respect their decisions in a different way. We process their love for us through a new lens. God is the same yesterday, today, and forevermore. That goes for His love too. As we grow deeper in relationship, we discover more about His ways. The Bible tells us that we cannot fully fathom how wide, long, high, or deep His love for us is (Eph. 3:18). Yet I am grateful that He gives us glimpses. We have the opportunity to discover the truth of His character and the impact of His love for, toward, and in us. Discovering His love for you is to experience who He is and how He behaves. You are invited to spend the next 30 days getting to know God as a father. As *your* Father.

His Ability

Years ago a hotel heiress was preparing to take her place in the higher ranks of the corporation. Many people thought she was receiving the leadership opportunity only because of who her family was. The masses were not confident in her ability to lead. In their eyes she was young and also just a woman. But she chose not to focus on what was being said but on approaching the task at hand. The young woman had access to her father, and she used it. Sitting in on meetings. Observing his habits. Willingly asking him for wisdom and help. She needed her father to be successful. It's been several years, and this young woman has continued to build credibility as a shrewd businesswoman. She regularly contributes to her family's brand portfolio.

Like the heiress, many of us have been given authority based on our connection to the head. But it's one thing to have authority and another thing to have the ability to carry out said authority. You may have accepted God's authority but not feel that you have the ability to carry it out. Allow the Lord to teach you how to shift your focus from your ability to *His* ability. We may experience limitations, but His power is limitless. When we choose to believe in God's Word, we're betting on Him, not ourselves! Don't allow unbelief to cripple you. God will be the power that stands tall above our weakness to fulfill everything that He desires in and through us!

Name the area of authority that God has called you to. In what areas do you need to shift your focus from self to Him?

———

The angel answered, "The Holy Spirit will come on you, and the power of the Most High will overshadow you."

LUKE 1:35 (NIV)

Prayer Prompt

Lord, I will shift my perspective. It's not about my limitations; it's about Your power . . .

He's with You

One of my sons was preparing for a Little League game. I could tell he was disappointed that his dad couldn't be with us because of another commitment. As my son prepared to play, I watched him look around one last time; he'd resolved that he'd have to play alone that day. Thanks to technology I was able to get Travis on a video call and take him to meet our son on the sideline. The look of recognition was followed by a sigh of relief and a huge grin. He wasn't alone. His daddy was there with him. My heart leapt at this moment.

Like my son, there have been many times where I thought I was just going to have to go at it alone in certain situations. And just as Travis is always there for our son, God has always been with me. I love when I get to encounter Him as Immanuel— God with us. It's an encouraging reminder of the benefits of being loved by a good Father.

Can I remind you today that God is with you? It doesn't matter what your situation may look like—He's present in it! In sickness or in health, He's with you. On the mountain or in the valley, He's with you. Remember, wherever He is, change is possible. Don't be discouraged by your situation. You have God on your side!

*In what area do you need to be
reminded that He's with you?*

These patriarchs were jealous of their brother Joseph, and they sold him to be a slave in Egypt. But God was with him.

ACTS 7:9

Prayer Prompt

Thank You, Lord, for always being here with me!
Teach me to be more aware of Your presence . . .

Where God Is

"I just want to be with you, Mommy," my son's tiny voice announced. I just wanted to go to the restroom, take a shower, and lie down. He brought his blanket into the bathroom and lay on the floor until I finished. As I went through my nightly routine, he sat on the bed, seemingly content to just be near me. In that moment I was reminded of what proximity between parent and child could look like and mean. He didn't want anything in particular. He had nothing to say. He just wanted to be near me.

I thought about all the times that I had shooed him away so I could get things done. How many times had he simply wanted to be near me with no other expectations? I quickly realized how this moment could be a mirror for my relationship with God. How many times had I hurried to get things done and missed the opportunity to be in His presence? More importantly, what seemingly mundane things had I missed because of my hurry to move on to the next thing?

Sometimes we're so in a rush to get to our "next." We're rushing to get our next job, relationship, or place. We find ourselves moving so quickly that we bypass God's location like missing a turn while driving. We've got to slow down. Don't rush to get anywhere that God isn't. Don't feel pressed to rush because you're going to miss out on something good. Good is wherever God is. Allow Him to be **Jehovah Shammah—the**

Lord Is There—in your life. You don't want to be anywhere the presence of the Lord isn't. Don't move ahead of Him! He'll get you to whatever is next in His timing.

What areas have you been rushing to? Where is Jehovah Shammah beckoning you instead?

———

You will show me the way of life, granting me the joy of your presence and the pleasures of living with you forever.

PSALM 16:11

—— *Prayer Prompt* ——

Lord, I want to be where You are! Teach me how to be content with where I am . . .

He Will Carry It

From the edge of the parking lot I could see the woman struggling to get all her groceries to the car. There were two kids with her, and they were doing what kids do: being silly. She was trying to ensure that the items didn't topple out of the basket while also trying to hold her kids' hands and help everyone safely cross the street. It was a lot, and she'd just let out a sigh of frustration when the store manager rushed to her aid. With one hand he grabbed the items that were balancing precariously, and with the other he steered the cart. By taking those things from her, he left the mother free to hold her children's hands. She was free to breathe and recompose herself. She was free because he'd stepped in to carry the load. When she got in the car, her eyes were damp with tears of relief.

We all have those moments when we have come to the end of ourselves and we are just *tired*. Let me remind you that God carries the weight of it all. There's relief that comes when we ask Him to provide strength when we feel weak. As we lean into Him and focus on His Word, we'll gain the necessary rest and needed energy! Sometimes the solution truly is rest.

Today, challenge yourself to not only pull closer to God but also trust Him as He carries the weight for you. Take a moment to breathe and recompose yourself. Relief is here.

Then Jesus said, "Come to me, all of you who are weary and carry heavy burdens, and I will give you rest."

MATTHEW 11:28

Prayer Prompt

God, thank You for carrying the weight of it all. You are my source of strength, especially when I am tired . . .

Quality Time

During His travels with the disciples, Jesus took the time to visit Martha and Mary personally. Martha busied herself doing all the things. I can imagine her whisking through the house, cleaning behind things Jesus probably wouldn't even notice. She was likely running back and forth to the kitchen preparing a multicourse meal. And looking to select the perfect wine to accompany the feast. All the while, Mary was sitting at Jesus' feet, chatting and listening. He was dropping knowledge, and Mary was scooping it up. Martha was likely yelling into the front room for help and muttering under her breath about how she had to do everything by herself. Talk about being big mad! She thought she was doing the right thing only to be told by Jesus that Mary was actually the one doing the right thing—spending time with Him, unbothered.

It may seem natural to want to keep ourselves busy doing things that we *think* the Lord wants us to do, but it's your attention that God wants most. God's love language is quality time. How can you truly know what God wants you to do if you don't stay close to Him? If we're not careful, we can end up doing things for God, without God. Don't be distracted! Time with God is always our top priority.

What are the many things that you need to put down to spend more time with God? Ask Him for strategies on how to worry less and encounter Him more.

But seek first the kingdom of God and his righteousness, and all these things will be added to you.

MATTHEW 6:33 (ESV)

Prayer Prompt

Daddy, I want to spend more time with You.
Help me to eliminate distractions . . .

He Empties to Fill

I keep returning to the theme of being overwhelmed because we've been conditioned to take on so much. As women our life containers are constantly filled with things to be done. There's always something to be finished, something to be carried, something to be handled. Those "somethings" aren't always ours either. They're from our bosses, our spouses, our children, our society. We just keep collecting things along our journeys, often unintentionally becoming bag ladies.

There were some things I carried around for so long that I forgot how heavy they were. I just kept pushing forward because that was what was expected of me. School expectations. Work responsibilities. Family requirements. But in my carrying, I didn't have room to hold all those things and the permission to go forth too. Eventually the burden became too much. God forced me to empty myself of every responsibility that was not my assignment—even things that I considered important. In that state of emptiness I realized how much I'd been clinging to certain things because of how they made me feel. There were other things that I thought heavily influenced what other people would feel about me. God required me to let those go too. And if I'm being honest, there were some things I was holding on to so tight that it took failures and disasters for me to let them go.

Sis, you're not alone when you find yourself in an empty season of asking, "God, why did You allow that to happen?" God empties us to fill us! He is loving enough to respond, saying, "My daughter, I allowed you to be emptied to create space for Me! I let that go wrong—to create space for Me. I let the betrayal happen—to create space for Me. I let you try with your best attempt and fail using your own ability—to create space for Me to fill you abundantly!"

What containers are you willing to voluntarily empty for Him to fill? What "nets" will you let down again to be filled by Him this time?

May the God of hope fill you with all joy and peace as you trust in him, so that you may overflow with hope by the power of the Holy Spirit.

ROMANS 15:13 (NIV)

Prayer Prompt

Lord, I want to be filled with You! You are welcome in all my empty spaces . . .

His Glory Alone

When my husband and I first started our church, he asked me to do the welcome at the first service. It was a simple, honorable request that brought a significant internal challenge for me. I wanted to do the welcome to support him, but I wasn't prepared. My mind rehearsed all the reasons why I couldn't do it. I didn't have prep time. I wasn't the spotlight person in our relationship. Famous friends would be joining us. The list unraveled, and I found myself crying in my mother's arms in a back room.

After some time in prayer and words of encouragement, I was ready. I accepted the permission that God had given me to be all that I could be. However, the full acceptance came only when I released the focus on myself. That night wasn't about Jackie. Or Travis, for that matter. It was about God and His glory. Shifting the focus from my inadequacies to God's glory alone was what transformed the overwhelm. I simply wanted to be obedient. A part of His glory being made manifest here on earth. I welcomed the people, and the service continued. We've had hundreds of services at Forward City since that first day in 2016. I've now lost count of the number of times I've welcomed God's people into His presence.

It's time for us to take our eyes off ourselves and allow our primary focus to be obeying and doing the will of the Father—no matter the cost! Let God take His rightful place as number one. We live for His glory alone. This is what life is all about—losing our life to gain real life in Christ!

What have you been holding back on that God is calling to be used for His glory?

By this my Father is glorified, that you bear much fruit and so prove to be my disciples.

JOHN 15:8 (ESV)

Prayer Prompt

Lord, I live for Your glory alone! I lay down my life so You may be glorified . . .

He Provides for Us

In the movie *The Pursuit of Happyness*, Will Smith's character, Chris Gardner, is seen going from place to place in hopes of securing work and the necessary provisions for his son. The film depicts Gardner going to extraordinary lengths in the midst of their financial despair and homelessness. From sleeping in transportation station restrooms to shelters and occasional hotels, this father continued pressing forward for his son. Eventually it all came together, and Gardner received a job offer that positioned him for a lifetime of financial success. I loved the update that appeared on the screen at the end of the movie, sharing that the real-life Chris Gardner eventually formed his own brokerage, later selling a minority stake in a multimillion-dollar deal. Talk about provision!

We may be facing scenarios where provision is needed. While we are doing our part, it's important that we also have faith for God to do His. Like Chris Gardner, He's a father who's going to continue making a way for us. In these moments we come to know Him as **Jehovah-Jireh—the Lord Who Provides**. It is up to us to stay the course that He has mapped out before us. When situations look dire, we must remind ourselves that He is Jehovah-Jireh. He is a good father, our provider. He will make a way out of no way. He will provide for us!

What are the areas in which you are trusting God to make provision?

And Abraham called the name of that place Jehovah Jireh: as it is said to this day, In the mount of the LORD it shall be seen.

GENESIS 22:14 (KJV)

Prayer Prompt

Daddy, I invite You to be Jehovah-Jireh in my life. I trust You to provide all that I need concerning . . .

His Healing

Every system in our body is connected. As a dentist, I can tell a lot about a person's overall health just by looking at their teeth. I can pick up on their habits from care to eating to sleeping. Cavities. Abscesses. Misalignment. Plaque buildup. Every symptom manifested in a person's mouth tells a story. Our bodies carry narratives about our well-being, including evidence of our emotional and mental states. In many cases our body's ailments are extensions of our internal health. Anxiety can cause us to grit our teeth in our sleep, which leads to jaw pain when we're awake. Stress can cause headaches, which can lead to poor eyesight and fatigue. Overwhelm can cause joint and muscle aches. How many times do we attempt to address our physical needs with the wrong course of treatment?

The list of our physical responses to life's circumstances can seem unending. But there is hope! We have an invitation to meet our Father God as **Jehovah Rapha—the Lord Our Healer**. He's our restorer. Jehovah Rapha has the cure to our *emotional* wounds. He is the balm for our *spiritual* bruises. He can repair the *physically* damaged things within us. It's up to us to trust Him as our healer and seek wisdom on how to proceed with treating the ailments.

What healing do you currently stand in need of? Make a list and invite God to intervene with wisdom and the appropriate solution.

For I am the LORD, who heals you.
EXODUS 15:26 (NIV)

Prayer Prompt

Father God, You are Jehovah Rapha.
I trust You to heal my . . .

He Is Your Peace

Have you ever noticed how some people can sleep anywhere? You know the ones—completely knocked out on buses, planes, and trains. They live in the peace of knowing they will get to their destination at the appropriate time. Children go to sleep in cars all the time, knowing that the driver has their safety in mind. Babies can rest peacefully in their parents' arms throughout an entire praise-and-worship service *unbothered*. Even Jesus slept in the bottom of a boat during a storm because He was at peace. In all of these examples, there is a combination of peace and trust at work. The trust is rooted in the belief that the destination will be reached.

This same peace is available to us as believers. When we remain in our role as beloved daughters, we get to experience our Abba in a new light. He becomes **Jehovah Shalom—the Lord Is Peace**.

Like babies in the arms of loved ones, we can rest in the peace of the Father's arms. That peace takes trust. And the wonderful thing is that Jehovah Shalom is trustworthy. We don't have to get worked up about how things are going to work out. We can trust that we will get to the other side of what we are facing. We can rest in the promise of peace that surpasses all understanding (Phil. 4:7). When you come against trying times and anxious moments, you have permission to call on the peace of the Lord.

You have the authority to speak to your storm and command, "Peace, be still" (Mark 4:39 KJV).

How have you experienced Jehovah Shalom in your life? In what areas do you need to accept His permission to live in peace?

Suddenly a furious storm came up on the lake, so that the waves swept over the boat. But Jesus was sleeping.
MATTHEW 8:24 (NIV)

Prayer Prompt

Jehovah Shalom, You are my peace! I believe
that I will live in Your peace that surpasses
all understanding concerning . . .

He Sanctifies Us

After joining a church, Alice didn't want to get involved with any of the ministries because of her past. She was ashamed of her upbringing and afraid that her previous decisions rendered her unworthy. Alice ran away from every opportunity for servant leadership because she didn't feel holy enough to hold the responsibilities. The same thing occurred when she met Christopher. He was interested in pursuing a relationship with her, but Alice couldn't see beyond her own mountain of guilt to embrace what he had to offer.

Through therapy and prayer she came to the acceptance that she was still a beloved daughter of the Lord, set apart and chosen. She recognized that God's call to righteousness was much more than moral purity—it was a lifestyle change based on His promise to transform her. The Lord promised Alice that He would complete the work in her until the day of Jesus Christ (Phil. 1:6). And she believed Him! The result was a deeper relationship with the Father and the start of a new, healthy relationship with Christopher.

God wants to sanctify us too. He wants us to experience Him as **Jehovah M'Kaddesh—the Lord Who Sanctifies**. However, this requires that we admit that sanctification is needed. I already know what picture comes to mind when I talk about being holy and sanctified. You picture long skirts, head coverings, and no makeup. You may even be thinking about being dressed in white with no earrings or adornment. Sis, I'm not talking about that! If you know me, then you know I love a good fashion trend and an edgy hairstyle. What I'm talking about is a posture of the heart. A submission of our desires and behaviors to His will. I'm talking about our daily choices. I'm talking about watching our mouths. And our thoughts too. As daughters of the King, we are called to holiness and sanctification. He wants to sanctify it all!

Identify the areas that you're willing to hand over to God for sanctification. Remember that no decision you've ever made changes His thoughts towards you and desire to sanctify you.

Keep my statutes and do them; I am the LORD who sanctifies you.

LEVITICUS 20:8 (ESV)

Prayer Prompt

Jehovah M'Kaddesh, I want to be sanctified by You . . .

He Knows

I shared with you earlier that each morning I spend time writing about where I am and how I am feeling. In one of those recent journal entries, I barely had the words to describe what I was going through. I felt heavy and uncertain. And the very thought of writing everything I was going through felt too overwhelming. My prayer that day began with a simple line, "Daddy, You know."

Have you ever had a day or moment like this? You are not alone. There will be days of frustration. There will be challenges. Thankfully we have access to **El Deah—the God of Knowledge**. As daughters of the King, we can experience His omniscience. We can rely on the proven characteristic of His knowledge.

God wants me to remind you today that *He knows*! He wants us to rest and relax in the truth that He knows every single detail concerning us. This relieves us of the temptation and resulting fatigue of trying to fix everything. Because He knows all, we don't have to. When we choose to give up the right to know it all and surrender, we rest easier, we release control, and we become a greater version of ourselves. We don't have to know everything; we just have to know the one who knows!

Spend time today reading and reflecting on Psalm 139:1-6.

You have searched me, LORD, and you know me.

PSALM 139:1 (NIV)

Prayer Prompt

Lord, You know! I surrender my need to know everything, and I depend on You . . .

His Truth

Lena had grown up with lots of transition throughout her childhood. To help cope with being the new kid so often, she began to finesse her stories in hopes of faster acceptance. Eventually Lena's stories became so elaborate that she had trouble separating fact from fiction. By the time she reached her early thirties, she was more confused than the little girl who made up stories to feel safe and foster a sense of belonging. She began to mistrust herself and others. When faced with a decision, Lena was never sure that she was making the right choice based on truth or emotions that she'd conjured up over time. The line between true and false had become blurred beyond recognition. Second-guessing became Lena's second nature.

As women we may not all have Lena's habit of stretching the truth, but many of us can identify with her uncertainty. We get lost in the barrage of what-ifs, suggestions, and possibilities.

The enemy is a master of hypothetical suggestions that don't lead to truth. He will ask, "What do you think they will think?" or "What will happen if you do things differently than you always have?" We often make the choice to change the way we are or the way we do things. This can feel scary, and the enemy will try to keep us stuck in the way we've always done things, keeping us from freedom. We begin to question our decision-making ability.

Do not be convinced or persuaded if God didn't say it. Any word in opposition to His Word is a lie and dangerous to believe. God's truth is present and has already been declared about you through His Word!

What lies and stories have you been holding on to that don't align with God's truth about you? Ask the Father to show you how to untangle yourself from those narratives.

Did God really say you must not eat the fruit from any of the trees in the garden?

GENESIS 3:1

Prayer Prompt

Daddy, if You didn't say it, I won't believe it. I will believe Your Word, for it is the truth . . .

What Is God Saying?

I know my husband's voice. I know my children's voices. Even if they're trying to tell me something from the other side of the house, I can often make out what they're saying. They know my voice just as well. "Please bring me the . . ." "Turn off the . . ."

Sometimes when we are not in close proximity, we still desire to communicate. In these moments, like at a ball game, I can shout my message and one of the boys or their friends will hear me. Based on the setting, I'm usually giving encouragement or instruction: "Keep going!" "You're doing such a great job." "You've got this!" They'll nod in understanding or repeat the words for confirmation.

I've got this. God is the same way with us. He's constantly speaking. Encouragement. Instruction. Conviction. Confirmation. It's up to us to hear what He's saying and put it into action. God's words are provision.

In a moment when God wants to provide what we need, it's vitally important that we align our words to what He desires to do. If He wants to heal someone, our words should speak healing! If He wants to send encouragement, speak encouraging words. When He's offering love, listen for His loving phrases. Don't fix your words to agree with what has happened to you or what others are saying. Agree with what God is saying. Saying exactly what God says provides us with what we need every time!

What is God saying to you today?
Repeat it. Agree with it.

———

Truly, I say to you, whoever says to this mountain, "Be taken up and thrown into the sea," and does not doubt in his heart, but believes that what he says will come to pass, it will be done for him.

MARK 11:23 (ESV)

Prayer Prompt

Father, help me to speak and agree
with what You say . . .

Promise Keeper

My son was excited about an event at school. As he asked my husband and me if we were attending for what seemed like the umpteenth time, I double-checked the family calendar and made the promise: we'll be there. He stopped asking and changed his language to agree with our promise of participation. The uncertainty was replaced by confirmation: "My mom and dad are coming." "I can't wait for you all to see . . ." "Dad, you're going to love . . ." I stood in awe of how quickly the transformation happened. All it took was a promise from his parents, and he believed! God has made many promises concerning our lives. We don't have to keep asking Him because He's already spoken. Instead, we are charged to come into agreement with His Word.

There is so much power in agreement! God is always speaking to you, the enemy's influence is always seeking to sway you, but the power is in *who* you agree with! Does your language align with what God says about you? The enemy can't do anything but lie, and God can't do anything but tell you the truth! Agree with God and disagree with every lie of the enemy!

God is a promise keeper. Dedicate time today
to write down the promises He's made to you,
directly and through Scripture. Highlight and give
thanks for the ones He's already fulfilled. Pray
regarding the ones you're still waiting to embrace.

For all of God's promises have been fulfilled in Christ
with a resounding "Yes!" And through Christ, our
"Amen" (which means "Yes") ascends to God for his glory.

2 CORINTHIANS 1:20

Prayer Prompt

Father, I agree with You! I believe Your promise to . . .

Just Like He Said He Would

I met a woman, Michelle, who struggled to keep healthy romantic relationships. When she was a young girl, her father often promised to visit or send her things. Each time she found herself sitting and waiting for him to come through on his word. And when he did, it was never as elaborate or complete as he'd promised. Michelle began to believe that she wasn't worthy of a man's full, intentional attention.

As she and I began to talk, we discussed what it would look like to have a man of his word in her life, romantically or otherwise. She couldn't imagine it. I could see how this was obstructing her ability to build a deeper relationship with Christ. Our next few meetings were focused on turning her attention away from her father and onto the Father. I challenged her to exchange her abandonment and rejection issues with her earthly father for love and truth from her heavenly Father.

I want to share the same truth with you. The Word of God cannot return to Him void! If He spoke a word over your life, you can believe it's gonna happen just as He said it would. He's not a man that He should lie, nor the son of man that He should have to repent (Num. 23:19). You can be sure that He will do it just as He said He would! He's going to come through for you.

Spend some time today praying for the areas where you have felt let down by man. It may have been for a job offer or a family opportunity. What is God's word to you concerning the matter?

———————

The LORD said to me, "You have seen correctly, for I am watching to see that my word is fulfilled."

JEREMIAH 1:12 (NIV)

———— *Prayer Prompt* ————

Lord, I receive what You've spoken over my life.
Show me how to take You at Your Word . . .

He's Trustworthy

The past few days of devotionals have focused on hearing and knowing the voice of God. On trusting Him. But let's be honest—hearing and knowing are different from trusting and acting. Someone once shared a social media video with me about a partner trust activity that requires one person to sit with an empty cup on their head. Their partner would stand behind them and throw a Ping-Pong ball or golf ball toward the cup. Their goal was to knock the cup off the person's head. Hilarity ensued as many people hit the person in the back of the head or completely missed the target altogether. But in all of the laughter, there were a few moments in which the person sitting in the chair was flinching. They were unsure of what was happening behind them and whether they could trust the person behind them not to bust them in the back of the head. Some of them were so nervous that they caused the cup to topple before the balls could be thrown. Trust mission failed.

How many times have we flinched or moved suddenly before God could execute the plans He has for us? Again, it's easy to know what He has said, but trusting and acting accordingly requires more of us.

God wants us to trust Him with all areas of our heart. He doesn't want us to depend on, rely on, or be controlled by our own understanding. Instead, we seek His will in all that we do so

He'll be able to guide us on the right path. He reminds us daily to not be impressed with our own wisdom but to fear the Lord and turn from evil. Today be encouraged that He is a Father who knows all, sees all, and wants what's best for us as His children.

Which areas of your life have you been afraid to trust God with? Confess them to Him today.

Trust in the LORD with all your heart
    and lean not on your own understanding;
in all your ways submit to him,
    and he will make your paths straight.
PROVERBS 3:5–6 (NIV)

Prayer Prompt

Father, continue Your work in me as I seek
Your will. I will trust in You today . . .

The Good Shepherd

James Baldwin's "The Ettrick Shepherd" is an inspirational depiction of a Scottish shepherd's commitment to his flock. While most shepherds employed the use of a rod and staff, James Hogg was a fourth-generation herder whose dog, Sirrah, helped him drive the flock from place to place. During a huge storm Hogg, Sirrah, and the flock were separated. After searching through the darkness and night with the help of other shepherds and lanterns, none of the seven hundred lambs had been found. Hogg began the journey home to tell his employer that all was lost. As they walked, the shepherds caught a glimpse of some lambs huddled together at the bottom of a ravine. When they went down into the steep gorge, they found many more lambs, along with Sirrah standing guard. All seven hundred of the flock were accounted for![4]

I don't know about you, but I've experienced quite a few storms in my life. Many of them felt like they were driving me further and further into the ravine. I found myself in the valleys, waiting. And even in the valley, God had me accounted for. He's a good shepherd.

Every day, God reminds us that even when we walk through the darkest valley, we don't have to be afraid because He's always beside us. He is **Jehovah Rohi—the Lord Our Shepherd**. He not only protects us but gives us complete comfort. He accounts for our whereabouts and well-being.

Remember that God is a protector and will always fight for us. The God of the mountain is the God of the valley! He is the Good Shepherd.

Even when I walk
    through the darkest valley,
I will not be afraid,
    for you are close beside me.
Your rod and your staff
    protect and comfort me.

PSALM 23:4

Prayer Prompt

Father, You walk beside me, and I don't
have to be afraid. I will walk through the
valley knowing You're with me . . .

He Is the Solid Rock

A young mother was a functioning alcoholic who tried time after time to find the best answer to her problems. One of the things she tried was different men, trying them on for size. How did he fit with the healing that she needed for her addiction? Too mean. Too soft. Abuse she didn't see coming. Irresponsible with money. Unbecomingly tight with the budgets. She changed her hair. She manipulated her appearance. Nothing seemed to work to get her the right man. Next on her list was to try on different religions and denominations. One was too rigid. Another felt wrong compared to how she'd grown up. Then there was the one that was over-the-top with habits and rituals. It was no surprise that when her daughter left home, she was totally confused about who she was and what she believed.

The daughter's response was to pursue a career that would allow her to climb the ranks quickly. She gained titles and earned promotions like few in the company had seen. Though successful in the workplace, this young woman was extremely guarded, rarely letting anyone into her personal life. After she was laid off during a company downsizing, the world and life she'd built came tumbling down, leaving her alone and unsure. She sank deep into a depression. Her anxiety rose, and it took significant efforts to get her back on track. She'd built her life on the security that she'd failed to receive as a child. Yet the security she'd built was unstable too. I sympathized with this young woman because I knew what it was like to try and course correct only to be let down. I, too, tried building parts of my life with my own shaking hands and flimsy materials. I had to release all of those things and rebuild my life on the firm promises of God.

God is our one and only firm foundation! When the waves come and the winds blow, you can be confident that your house will stand. He is a steady place. He is an anchor. Let this be a reminder that when you're experiencing anxiety or depression or anything that knocks you off balance, you have a *solid rock* to stand on!

What have you built your life on? In which areas do you need a new, firm foundation in Christ?

> For who is God except the LORD?
> Who but our God is a solid rock?
> PSALM 18:31

Prayer Prompt

Abba, thank You for being my solid rock!
Teach me how to build my life on You . . .

Easy to Please

Pam started her people-pleasing habits early in life. As a result, the pattern continued into adulthood. Everything she did was rooted in pleasing others, from work to church to her daughter's activities. Nothing was for herself. Pam lost sight of her own identity in her people-pleasing. How many times have we, too, gone to great lengths trying to please others? Maybe it was the way we wore our hair. Perhaps we changed our major in college. It may be that we tamped down our true feelings and opinions to make someone else feel better about themselves in a difficult exchange.

The good news is that God doesn't require any of these things to be loved by Him. In fact, He's easy to please and gives us clear instruction on what it takes to please Him—faith. That's it! Faith is confidence and assurance in a person or situation. Faith is about belief and trust. God desires that in all things we remain full of faith. We must wage war on doubt! When you drown out the voice of doubt, you can hear the voice of God. We walk by faith and not by sight (2 Cor. 5:7). So if what you see is causing you to doubt, allow God to reveal His truth to you. Don't doubt God—doubt your doubts! Choose the easy route; have faith.

What areas have you been trying to please others in?
How can you turn those areas over to God in faith?

And it is impossible to please God without faith. Anyone
who wants to come to him must believe that God exists
and that he rewards those who sincerely seek him.

HEBREWS 11:6

Prayer Prompt

Lord, I will no longer doubt You! Teach me
how to trust and place my faith in You . . .

He's Fighting for Me

It's so easy to get worked up over circumstances and situations. In some cases we've inherited fear. In others, frustration builds as we survey what's going on around us. We feel powerless and begin allowing fear and frustration to drive our actions. Simply put, we panic. And in the fight of our lives, we start flailing our arms. Like an inexperienced fighter, we start throwing punches that aren't landing. We're moving our feet yet not getting out of the path of the blows that the opponent is throwing at us. Not only are we getting pummeled, we are quickly getting tired.

The problem is we're in the wrong fight class. We are lightweights trying to take on heavyweights. These mismatched battles can cause so much fear to rise in us. In these lopsided encounters we have several possible actions to help us. First, we can do the training necessary to meet the fight-class requirements. Second, we can tag in a partner who's got a better chance at winning.

Sis, we can walk through life with so much fear. We can think that we will never be truly free of the bondage we're currently in. It seems like the only option is to be in darkness or bound by our circumstances. We're in the scuffles being worn down. But it doesn't have to be this way. Fear and frustration are not our portion. In these moments we have an opportunity to meet **Jehovah Gibbor—the Lord, the Mighty Warrior.** Jehovah

Gibbor is mightier than any opposition and situation we face. Today the Father is simply saying, "I will fight for you; just stay calm." Do not be afraid—just stand still and watch the Lord rescue you today! Tag Him in. He's ready to fight for you!

Think of the battles you've been trying to fight recently. Which one is the Father asking you to let Him fight on your behalf?

The LORD himself will fight for you. Just stay calm.

EXODUS 14:14

Prayer Prompt

Father, today I choose to stand on Your promises as
You fight for me. It's not over until You say so . . .

Guaranteed Victory

When the final buzzer rang, the stadium erupted into deafening cheers. Some of the players pointed their fingers up to the sky. A few of their family members and friends burst into tears. The road to the playoffs had been challenging, but this moment of victory proved the team to be true champions. As the award was brought to the sidelines, a banner was lowered from the rafters. Fans in the stands howled with excitement and waved their own banners in celebration.

During an interview the coach calmly stated that he'd expected his team to win all along. He'd seen their victory in his dreams. He'd envisioned the banner hanging in the rafters. In the coach's mind there was no other outcome available aside from a guaranteed victory. He'd convinced his players of the same. As a result they worked together to deliver on the mission. God is like that about our assignments. Whatever our call on this earth, the Lord has already declared us victorious.

One of the characteristics of God centers on His protection and guidance. Moses referred to Him as **Jehovah Nissi—the Lord Our Banner**. This reference is a reminder that God leads and guides us, even in battle. Even when it looks like a situation isn't going in our favor, His banner still waves and covers us. Our end is always a win despite what the process may look like in between. Our God has never lost a battle, and He never will.

Even the things that look like losses are just a setup for greater wins. Don't give up; you're on the winning team! Victory is guaranteed for you.

What circumstance do you need to declare God's victory over in your life today? Envision the victory, then write down what you see.

But thanks be to God, who gives us the victory through our Lord Jesus Christ.

1 CORINTHIANS 15:57 (ESV)

Prayer Prompt

Thank You, God, for being able to do all things except fail. I always win with You . . .

The God of Abundance

Television in the 1950s showed the likes of June Cleaver living solely dedicated to serving her family as a stay-at-home wife and mother. As society changed, more women began working outside the home. A tug-of-war began, with people sharing their ideas on whether women could succeed as wives and mothers with jobs. Could they have it all? Could they have it all and be happy? Then the books, programs, and memes started coming out: *You can have it all if . . . The key to having it all is . . . Having it all requires . . .* And as with anything, there were always naysayers: *When you try to have it all, _____ happens. Having it all means losing . . . It's impossible to have it all and . . .* With all these caveats and compromises, can women really have it all and be happy?

I'm here to tell you that you can. You can have *all* that God says you can have! If He called you to it, He will equip you to handle it. The challenge with attempting to have it all is that we become overwhelmed. Many times when we are overwhelmed, it's not because of what the Father has placed on us but what the world tells us to go get. Everything is pointing to hustle culture, and while that may work for some people for a period of time, it's not a sustainable lifestyle. Sometimes we need to pause and evaluate who or what is influencing us. Is it the Instagram model who chose the best photo to post out of fifteen takes? Is it a celebrity with a team of people surrounding her to execute all of the things? There are good things, and there are God things. The Bible tells us that the blessings of the Lord make us rich and add no sorrow (Prov. 10:22). When your life is filled with God things, you can have it all in abundance. You're graced to handle all that *He* has called you to!

Are the things you're pursuing just good things or truly God things?

And God is able to bless you abundantly, so that in all things at all times, having all that you need, you will abound in every good work.

2 CORINTHIANS 9:8 (NIV)

Prayer Prompt

Father, teach me how to handle all that You've given me. Show me how to let go of what You haven't called me to . . .

He Has Overcome

Beloved sister, we are not called to be damsels in distress. We have been chosen to live lives of unconditional love, permission, and faith. Of course, living lives of permission and faith does not mean that we will not experience trials and sorrows. Quite the opposite—we *will* go through them! The Bible tells us so. But how we decide to face those trials and sorrows makes the difference. If you're like me when facing a specific challenge, you just want to get it over with. *Please, Lord, just let me get through this in one piece.*

As beloved daughters we don't have to take the position of beggar or victim. We have a Savior who has already gone through the hard things. Moreover, He is interceding on our behalf. And if you really want to go in, simply think of the fact that we are co-heirs with Jesus! This means outcomes have already been decided because of who we're connected to. Everything He has, we have access to.

The Bible says to take heart, because Jesus has overcome the world (John 16:33). The battle over our many trials and sorrows has already been won! Therefore, whatever you are facing today has a position of defeat because your position is *victory*. When Jesus overcame the world, He overcame your situation, too, no matter how tough it may seem.

*What are you currently facing that can
benefit from both allowing Jesus to be the
overcomer and accepting His peace?*

I have told you all this so that you may have peace in me.
Here on earth you will have many trials and sorrows.
But take heart, because I have overcome the world.

JOHN 16:33

Prayer Prompt

Thank You, Lord, for overcoming the world!
I will hand my situation over to You, knowing
that You can overcome that too . . .

Abundant Life Giver

I'm making it. How many times have you responded to someone's inquiry about your well-being this way? I know I have. At times this feels like the only response that will keep things short, sweet, and moving. Other times, it's been the only response that will keep the dams of frustration and overwhelm from breaking. The problem with the "I'm making it" and "I'm surviving" ways of living are that you're not really living. Existing, surviving, and striving are not the way of life we are destined to experience as daughters of the king. We have access to all the things that help us to thrive. We have access to a full life. We have permission to experience God's life-giving freedom.

He doesn't desire for us to just make it through. He wants us to truly live in abundance! Truly living God's way is winning! Recognize that the enemy wants us to take loss after loss. Stealing our joy. Killing our dreams. Destroying our families. No more! God has an answer for that! Trustworthy promises. Revived hope. Whole families. The Lord came for us to have abundant lives! Abundance of joy. Abundance of healing. Abundance of finances and resources. Abundance of love. Abundance belongs to us. We have permission to live abundantly!

Set aside time today to identify the areas the enemy has been attacking. What does abundant living in those areas look like? Write it down.

The thief comes only to steal and kill and destroy. I came that they may have life and have it abundantly.
JOHN 10:10 (ESV)

Prayer Prompt

I serve a life-giving God! Thank You for giving me an abundant life in You . . .

Teacher of Rest

When I had each of my boys, the women surrounding me offered the same advice—sleep while the baby is sleeping. Early on I couldn't imagine what that looked like. How in the world was I going to sleep when there was so much to be done? Laundry. Housecleaning. Wifeying. The list seemed endless.

A good girlfriend brought it into perspective: "Jackie, God created an entire world and still took time to rest." Touché. I took that information to heart and began to examine other examples of rest throughout the Bible. The ones that caught my attention were the moments that Jesus took to rest. He was running a ministry with an extended travel itinerary and a full staff of disciples who, I am sure, were at times acting like our demanding family members and work colleagues. And Jesus still found time to rest. No, let me correct that. He made time to rest. On His way to Galilee, He pulled over in Samaria to rest at the well (John 4). In the middle of the day no less! After a full healing tour, He got in a boat and slept through an entire storm (Matt. 8). In all that was on His to-do list, Jesus followed the Lord's command to rest. He trusted that the assignments would still be fulfilled, even if He rested. Jesus modeled the trust that is rest.

Do you trust God enough to actually rest? When was the last time you took a day to just devote to the Lord? I'm learning that God knows how to best get all that He's put inside me, out!

These cycles of unrest and burnout we go through can all be linked to us not setting aside time to honor the Lord with our rest. Give God your trust by taking time to rest!

Pull out your calendar. Schedule a few hours of rest within the next seven days.

Observe the Sabbath day by keeping it holy, as the LORD your God has commanded you.

DEUTERONOMY 5:12

Prayer Prompt

Lord, help me to rest in You! I want to trust You enough to take a day to rest . . .

His Reward

I saw a video on Instagram where a son told his mom he needed cash. The mother offered her young son twenty dollars if he could find it wherever she placed it in the house. No work required. No catch. If he found it within three days, the reward was his to keep. If three days passed without him locating it, the money went back to her. For three days she captured her son looking all through the house. He looked under the couch. She showed him peering on top of the kitchen cabinets. He leaned into the washing machine and the oven. After combing through drawers, checking the garage, and exhausting every hiding place he could think of, the son had not found the money. Spoiler alert—she'd hidden it in his deodorant. He was so preoccupied with finding the reward that he wasn't keeping current with his daily responsibilities. Or maybe he was being a typical adolescent boy needing constant reminders of the basics. Either way he missed his reward.

As believers we have some basics to live by too. We are encouraged to pray without ceasing (1 Thess. 5:17) and to seek God's kingdom first (Matt. 6:33). We are reminded in multiple places throughout Scripture to seek Him (e.g., 2 Chron. 7:14; Jer. 29:13; Lam. 3:25). That's where the reward is found—in seeking Him. He is the reward!

How many times have we missed the reward by looking

in the wrong place? Make sure you live to please your Father in heaven! Don't seek the praises of others. When you need people to reward you with their likes and acceptance, that's all the reward you will receive (Matt. 6:2–4; Gal. 1:10). However, when you pray you gain the attention of heaven! God desires to reward you privately before you receive anything publicly. Seek the face of God before you seek the praises of men. Your reward will be far greater!

In what areas of your life have you been looking for your reward in the wrong place?

For they loved the praise of men more than the praise of God.

JOHN 12:43 (NKJV)

Prayer Prompt

Father, I choose to pray and seek Your face. Help me seek Your reward more than that of man . . .

He's Responsive

Melody kept calling her big brother's name. Theo continued to ignore her. She jumped in front of the television only to be met with the fury of his frustrated words. He didn't want to hear or see her. He was too busy to give her the attention she was seeking. This was not the first or the last time that Melody would be ignored. Over time she internalized people's choices to ignore her and became more introverted. She stopped asking for help. If she couldn't figure out something on her own, it simply would not get done.

Does any of this sound familiar? Sometimes we believe that the way people around us behave is the way God behaves. We begin to give Him the silent treatment in hopes that we never feel the sting of unresponsiveness from Him. But our relationship with Him doesn't work like that. We can't let the fear of being ignored prevent us from experiencing the abundance of His love. God is not like people. He is always paying attention to us!

We can't fulfill God's will without Him! We must seek Him in prayer to gain clarity on His agenda for our lives as His beloved daughters each day. We must lay down our emotions, feelings, and tiredness to consistently pursue communication with Him. In prayer we find out what He desires for us and how we can partner with Him to bring it into the earth. "Thy kingdom come, thy will be done" (Matt. 6:10 KJV) happens in prayer.

Ask the Lord what His will is for you.

Give Him space and time to respond.

The righteous cry out, and the LORD hears them; he delivers them from all their troubles.

PSALM 34:17 (NIV)

Prayer Prompt

Lord, teach me how to pray! I trust that not only will You hear me, but You will respond . . .

He's a Restorer

Beverly was a woman in her late fifties who I had the pleasure of meeting. During our conversation she shared that she had lost several things over the years due to circumstances and situations—some in her control, others not. Marriage, family, and work had required her to put a few dreams on the back burner, including school and travel. Yet when she spoke of those dreams, I saw a glimmer of excitement in her eyes. Based on her demeanor, it appeared that some of the lost dreams were still very much alive in her heart. As we continued to talk, Holy Spirit offered a fresh perspective on those old dreams. He began to show her ways that she could complete her education and use it as a way to travel. He made it all make sense, regardless of her age and accomplishment—both which Beverly felt were hindrances. We reconnected about six months later, and she shared how she was in a new place. God had been restoring things that she thought were long out of her reach.

As with Beverly, God wants to do new things in your life. He desires to restore things that you think are long destroyed. Not only that, He wants to restore those things in abundance (Joel 2:25–26).

God wants to give you new fire, new perspective, and new grace. The common challenge is that the Father's ways of restoration and newness don't always look like we expect. The Israelites had to eat manna in the wilderness. The widow woman had to fill empty jars with oil. Moses had to strike a rock with a staff. Ezekiel had to speak to a valley of bones. But after each of these examples of obedience, God showed himself a mighty restorer. To experience the new you must do something new!

Perhaps God is urging you to complete the application. Maybe He's calling you to make a phone call to that person (yeah, that one). Ask God today what action you must take to experience His newness and restoration.

Then the LORD your God will restore your fortunes and have compassion on you and gather you again from all the nations where he scattered you.

DEUTERONOMY 30:3 (NIV)

Prayer Prompt

Daddy, reveal to me the things that I thought were lost or dead. Instruct me on the ones You desire to restore . . .

The Doorman

On a popular 1970s sitcom the Jeffersons moved to a fancy high-rise as a symbol of their economic success. Their new residence had a doorman, Ralph, who visited their apartment on occasion. Ralph brought up the mail, delivered packages, and carried bags. He opened the doors for easy entry. His role conveyed the level of privilege the Jeffersons had accessed with their move.

A doorman's primary responsibility is opening doors for residents to enter and exit. If there is a visitor, he has to grant access for them to go beyond the lobby. For this reason having a doorman can be viewed as more than a luxury and also a necessity for security. He remembers the names and faces of those who belong. He's well aware of those who are strangers seeking entry for distraction or destruction. Similarly, our God is an attentive doorman.

As Christians, we are very aware of open and closed doors in our lives. However, the real question is if this is an open door from God—should you walk through it? The job? The boyfriend? The business opportunity? It's essential to remember that the enemy can also open doors, just as Satan opened doors for Jesus (Matt. 4:3–10). Woman of Freedom, that's when stepping out on faith gets tricky! *Who is the doorman, or guardian, on duty? When I step through this door, what will I have access to? Who or what will have access to me? Am I entering a restricted area?* We need discernment and sensitivity to consider the doors open to us. Keep listening to your Father to know which opportunities are from Him and which ones are not.

Identify the doors that have been open to you lately. Which of them are from God for your effective work?

. . . because a great door for effective work has opened to me, and there are many who oppose me.

1 CORINTHIANS 16:9 (NIV)

Prayer Prompt

Lord, give me discernment on which opportunities to take. Thank You for keeping me safe from the enemy's plans . . .

Discovering His Love

Think back over the last 30 days. Hopefully you've come to a better understanding of who God is and how He shows up in a variety of ways. Protector. Healer. Worthy of trust. Before continuing to the final collection of devotions, take time to reflect on how discovering His love for you has unfolded.

- The attributes of the Father I admire most are . . .
- My position as a beloved daughter provides access to . . .
- I feel more connected to the Lord when . . .
- I'd like to know more about God as . . .

PART 3

Remaining in His Love

To live loved is to be fully free.
DR. JACKIE GREENE, *PERMISSION TO LIVE FREE*

Remaining in love is not a onetime thing. It is a continuous choice and constant commitment. I pray that whether you are just beginning the journey or have been walking with the Father for a long time, this final section will help you remain in love.

I end each of my *Permission* broadcasts by asking my guests, "What's the secret sauce for this season?" This is an opportunity for the guest to give me their secret ingredient or principle that is helping them navigate life. Each response is a reminder that we are constantly becoming. That means there is room for growth and change—we are becoming who God gave us permission to be. The closing 30 days of devotions are all about remaining in love with who God is and who we are in Him. In this season the secret sauce includes two ingredients: accepting permission to be loved as God's daughter and operating in the obedience and authority given to us as joint heirs with Christ.

Obey His Instruction

If you have children or have been around them, you know how interesting it can be to get them to follow instructions. They certainly have minds and wills of their own. A woman I know tells her children to "follow instructions the first time given." Older adults used to say, "Don't make me have to tell you again." Now, with boys of my own, I understand. I often desire for the instruction to be done without question, back talk, or hesitation.

Similarly God wants us to obey His instructions the first time given. Two of the clearest examples of this are when God gave Abraham and Jonah instructions. Abraham immediately followed the instructions and set off to sacrifice Isaac (Gen. 22). Jonah, on the other hand, received His instructions and tried to outrun God (Jonah 1).

Abraham's immediate obedience resulted in generational blessings. Jonah's immediate quest for his own will brought about a storm, disrupting his life and the lives in the ship with him. He ended up spending three days in the belly of the fish before being delivered, and then God had to speak to Jonah a second time. The reward for his eventual obedience was the saving of Nineveh, a very large city (Jonah 3:10).

What if the key to your next breakthrough is in your obedience to the Lord? When God gives you instruction, it's because He's gone ahead of you! He knows what steps are necessary to obtain victory. All you need to do is trust Him enough to obey. Obey Him and watch how He fulfills His promise to you!

What instructions have you recently received from the Lord? (It doesn't have to be a verbal command; the instruction may have come through a response to something you read in the Word or a devotional.) How have you been responding— with immediate obedience or stormy hesitation?

The disciples went and did as Jesus had instructed them.
MATTHEW 21:6 (NIV)

Prayer Prompt

Father, I will obey Your instruction.
Teach me Your will for my life . . .

Be Transformed

Gabby badly wanted a promotion. But she was still showing up late for work most days. And if conflict arose with a coworker, she retreated to the defensive tone and language that had been with her since childhood. As a result, she wasn't taken seriously in her requests for consideration. One day a more senior woman in the office, Cheryl, invited her out to lunch to discuss her goals. During the meal Gabby recited her frustrations. She'd gone to school. She'd taken the additional professional development courses. She worked overtime. Yet no one seemed to recognize her efforts.

Cheryl explained that it had been great watching Gabby climb the ranks since her early position as a receptionist. However, much of her behavior and performance in the office still resembled that of a temporary receptionist rather than a leading manager. Cheryl encouraged Gabby to transform her mind and actions to match that of a leader. Was there a better way to deliver information? What time management tools could be helpful on her journey? While she had all of the book and classroom knowledge, she needed a full transformation to achieve her goals.

Gabby accepted that she had to change her mindset and her thinking to change the outcome at work. After six months of consistency, Gabby was up for promotion. There was no more back-and-forth in her actions and attitude when she didn't get her way. Her promotion was approved.

If you change your mind but you don't change your life, your mind will change again. Be transformed! Allow the powerful revelation of who God is to influence you to change your life, habits, and desires. God wants to do something new in us, but we must allow Him to transform us by changing the way we think so that we may learn His will for us and live it out!

Identify the areas where you've been stuck in your thinking and actions. What changes can you make to move forward?

Don't copy the behavior and customs of this world, but let God transform you into a new person by changing the way you think. Then you will learn to know God's will for you, which is good and pleasing and perfect.

ROMANS 12:2

Prayer Prompt

Lord, I'm ready to be transformed! I will no longer go back to the way things used to be . . .

Can They Tell?

I love reflecting on how personal Moses' relationship with God was. There's one particular story in the book of Exodus that I'm drawn to because Moses got to spend one-on-one time with God on the mountain. When he came down from their encounter, Moses' face was radiant. It was so bright that Aaron and the Israelites were afraid to come near him! Moses eventually developed a routine of placing a veil over his face when speaking to the people and uncovering his face when speaking with God. The Israelites knew that anytime he came out with a glowing face, he'd been in the presence of the Lord.

Can people tell that you've been in the presence of the Lord? When people come around you, there should be something different about you. Maybe you respond to challenges differently. Perhaps love is your tone. Are you accompanied by a specific type of courage? After spending time in the presence of the Lord, others should be able to tell. Your friends, family, and coworkers should feel a shift when you walk in a room! Your personal devotion should have an external effect! There should be a remnant, or overflow, of your time in His presence. Be aware of what your presence brings. Bring Jesus with you!

Is there a characteristic you have that does not reflect the likeness of God?

———

But you will receive power when the Holy Spirit has come upon you, and you will be my witnesses in Jerusalem and in all Judea and Samaria, and to the end of the earth.

ACTS 1:8 (ESV)

Prayer Prompt

Lord, I want my life to reflect You. I pray that when people see me, they see You . . .

Wait on Him

For a large portion of my life, I wore extensions. This required extended amounts of time in the beauty salon, and there was always a wait associated with the process. Waiting during the shampoo, detangling, and drying. Waiting through the braiding and installation. Waiting for the cut and style. Waiting. Waiting. Waiting. And no matter how long the wait, chances were that I was going to still keep sitting there. Why? Because I knew the outcome. I knew that I'd be looking good!

We get accustomed to waiting in certain scenarios—new music releases, new shoe drops, new book launches. Yet when it comes to waiting on God, it's a bit harder. We want Him to do the thing now. Here's the deal: we already know the outcome. All of the elements, including the wait, are working together for our good. We know that He has given us hope and a future. He's going to complete the work He started and perfect all the things concerning us. And we still get antsy while waiting? One thing I have found is that anything premature has complications. This has taught me to trust the Lord's timing more and more!

The only thing that brings us favor is God. His presence is the difference maker! Wait on the Lord. In jobs, relationships, business decisions, and everything else, we sometimes have to wait. Whatever it may be, don't move ahead of Him. Daughter, you can trust His timing! Decide today that you won't make another move without Him. We don't want the promise without the *promise keeper*!

What are the things that you have been waiting on? How will having His favor accompany them make the arrival more enjoyable?

The LORD is good to those who wait for him,
to the soul who seeks him.
LAMENTATIONS 3:25 (ESV)

Prayer Prompt

Lord, You are the one who brings favor!
Teach me how to wait on You . . .

Put in Work

Going to the gym hasn't always been something I love. However, I recognize that to meet some of my health goals, I have to put in work. I don't want to simply appear good-looking; I want to be physically fit too. That means doing cardio exercises that will strengthen my heart. It means doing the work to burn fat and build muscle. Putting in the work away from the gym is also necessary. I love a good batch of fries covered in ketchup, but I can't eat them daily and still expect to see and feel results. Sometimes the only work required is simply opening my mouth to say no to the things that don't align with my fitness goals. The same is true for other areas of our lives. There is work necessary to advance in our assignments.

Learning about spiritual disciplines will give you everything you need to take small steps towards living a more disciplined life with God. Spiritual disciplines include Bible reading, prayer, fasting, worship, meditation, and much more. These aren't just mundane tasks; spiritual disciplines are how we remain with the Father. They're our response to His love for us! I've found that putting in the spiritual work not only strengthens my soul but carries over to other areas of my life. When I am strong in my faith, my faith pushes me to do the work required to get results in other areas of my calling—my marriage, my parenting, my home, my career. It's all about putting in the work. If we've got to work anyway, we might as well put in the work with Him!

*Take out your calendar. Block off specific
work time this week dedicated to your
spiritual goals. Follow through.*

No discipline seems pleasant at the time, but painful.
Later on, however, it produces a harvest of righteousness
and peace for those who have been trained by it.

HEBREWS 12:11 (NIV)

Prayer Prompt

Lord, I want to become more disciplined
in my walk with You. Show me how to
pray, fast, and read Your Word . . .

Reach for Him

When I think of reaching, a few images come to mind. The first is of a toddler reaching because they want to be picked up. Even without words, their reach speaks of what they want or need. The second image is an older woman in the grocery store. She has her eye on the specific item that she needs, yet even when she stands on her tiptoes, she's unable to reach it. She has to ask a passerby to help her. And the final image is a person climbing on one of those practice rock-climbing walls. To get higher up the wall, they must release the rung they're holding on to, reach for the next one, and pull themselves up.

In each of these examples I'm reminded that a person is trying to achieve a goal. Living the abundant life God has promised requires us to reach upward. We have to reach for Him.

God is our Father and Savior! He wants to give us a higher, broader view. We can see more when we are elevated. There are moments we will need to be saved from our own thoughts, life happenings, worldly demands, and unexpected situations. And as we get closer to God's promises, there are certain things that we must let go of to reach for Him. When we let go, our hands are free to grasp the next rung of support and elevation.

God desires to be there for you every single day. He wants to put things within reach that are out of our own comfort and achievement level. He wants to give us full access. There are certain things that we must let go of in order to reach for Him. When we let go of those things, our hands are free to grasp the next rung of support and elevation. You don't have to be strong for your Father—it's okay to need Him! He can lift you. He can reach what's beyond your grasp. He can pull you up from the lower place.

In what areas have you failed to reach for Him because you felt weak or that a desire was totally out of reach? Your encouragement today is to reach for Him!

Each time he said, "My grace is all you need. My power works best in weakness." So now I am glad to boast about my weaknesses, so that the power of Christ can work through me.

2 CORINTHIANS 12:9

Prayer Prompt

Father, I need You! When life hits me, I
won't be afraid to reach for You . . .

Rest in His Word

As beloved daughters, part of our inheritance comes through our ability to rest. But as women that can be hard to do. When creditors are calling. When the school is demanding our attention. When we are looking for a solution. We've been conditioned by society to figure it out, to make a way. But in this season of love, God is giving us permission to rest in His Word. I keep coming back to this concept of rest because it is essential for us to be well rested to carry out our assignments. We need rest to know how to answer the calls coming our way. We need rest to support our families. We need rest to hear clearly from God.

Whatever you're facing today, the Lord wants to teach you to abide and rest in Him and His Word. This means that worrying all night will not leave you refreshed for the tasks of tomorrow. Worrying will not add a day to your life (Luke 12:25–26). Understand that God can do more in a moment than we can do in our lifetime. God's word over your life will accomplish what it was sent out to do. *Rest* because it's already done!

Spend time today reflecting on what God has said concerning you. List those truths. Pray over them, confessing that His Word will come to pass in your life.

———

So is my word that goes out from my mouth:
It will not return to me empty,
but will accomplish what I desire
and achieve the purpose for which I
sent it.

ISAIAH 55:11

Prayer Prompt

Father, I thank You for Your Word, which gives me life.
Teach me how to abide and rest in what You say . . .

Live Out the Word

Thinking ahead is a skill that we are taught as part of critical thinking. In various settings we even receive rewards for our ability to predict outcomes and beat our opponents. I think of this most often when it comes to those competition reality shows like *The Amazing Race*. Teams are doing everything they can to beat their foes to the end point. There's always at least one team that seems to be stuck in a maze of directions, never to reach the finish line. And then there's usually a team that thinks they are so smart at outwitting the others that they end up skipping steps or missing important directions. I always laugh because the race would be much easier if they simply took the time to read and understand the directions before they took off running.

Our lives are similar. God gives us directions, and we find ways to overcomplicate what He's said. A story in 2 Kings 5 illustrates this perfectly. Naaman went to Elisha for instructions on healing. When he was told to dip in the Jordan River seven times, Naaman became angry. He had different expectations for the process and the outcome. Yet his healing was tied to his ability to follow the word given to him.

What is the last instruction that the Father gave you? Sometimes we get caught in cycles simply because we didn't obey the last instruction He gave us! It's not enough to just know His Word; we have to live it out each and every day. Living what we know can help us get out of the cycle of constantly repeating the same things. He's given us instructions on our finances. He's given us instructions on parenting and relationships. It is up to us to live out His Word obediently. Sis, to remain in this season of love we can't just be hearers of the Word—we must be doers (James 1:22–25). Believe and live out His Word!

What was the last instruction that the Father gave you? Do it.

My counsel for you is simple and straightforward: Just go ahead with what you've been given. You received Christ Jesus, the Master; now *live* him. You're deeply rooted in him. You're well constructed upon him. You know your way around the faith. Now do what you've been taught. School's out; quit studying the subject and start *living* it! And let your living spill over into thanksgiving.

COLOSSIANS 2:6–7 (MSG)

Prayer Prompt

God, I will live out Your Word! Each and every day, teach me how to obey Your instruction . . .

Recognize What You Have

When Travis and I were dating, I had a mindset that I would be fine with or without him. Because I was secure in my God-given identity, I was not dependent on finding a man to complete me. I was whole with what I had. It would ultimately be this confidence that attracted him to me for the long term. I knew who I was, which lifted a weight off him to not have to build me up. Additionally, if I wasn't aware of who I was and sensitive to who I was becoming, I wouldn't have written my first book. I wouldn't have written this one. I wouldn't have started the Permission Room Mentorship Group.

"Comparison is the thief of joy." This powerful phrase attributed to former president Theodore Roosevelt holds so much weight. Sometimes we can be so busy looking at what others are doing that we lose sight of what we are called to do and who we are called to be. We look at other people (especially on social media) and immediately wish we had more, looked different, sounded different, and the list goes on.

Every time the enemy comes, he has a purpose: to steal, kill, and destroy. If he's coming, it must mean that you carry something worthy and valuable enough to be taken or stolen! Don't overlook all that God has poured inside of you. Recognize what you have! Hold on to it tightly. Your assignment is unique to you. Your gifts and callings excel because of your approach, even if it's similar to someone else's. No one can answer the call like you can.

Make a list of the callings, gifts, talents, and abilities that God has put in your hands. Keep it nearby as a reminder when doubt, insecurity, and imposter syndrome try to creep in and steal your confidence.

The thief comes only to steal and kill and destroy; I have come that they may have life, and have it to the full.
JOHN 10:10 (NIV)

Prayer Prompt

I recognize the good things that You have placed in and around me. I won't continue to overlook all that You've poured into me . . .

Use Your Voice

In the popular movie *Girls Trip*, Regina Hall's character, Ryan Pierce, was invited to speak at Essence Fest. By the time she was supposed to take the stage, a number of things had fallen apart—her picture-perfect marriage and a longtime friendship included. She had a few choices. She could go on with the planned script and pretend everything was okay when it wasn't. She could run away and abandon her audience. Or she could use her voice to share authentically about the realities of her "perfect life." Spoiler alert: she used her voice to share her truth. Each day you and I are given the same opportunities when it comes to our less-than-perfect experiences. We can continue faking it until we make it to go along with the status quo. We can abandon our assignments and all of those who are attached to them. Or we can share from a place of victorious vulnerability.

You may not be a pulpit preacher or stadium speaker, but there is so much power in sharing your testimony! Don't allow the enemy to hold shame, guilt, and condemnation over you. Use your voice to take your power back. That's how you overcome! Your story, your triumph—they're weapons. To be an effective warrior, you must know how to use your tools properly. This includes your voice. No matter what it looks like, you must declare your truth. Use your voice, sis! Share the ways that you've been made free. Announce the things that have already been done. Declare the things you're expecting to see turned around for your good. Speak of the goodness of the Lord in your life. Use your voice!

What has the Lord delivered you from? What has He snatched you out of? Share your story with someone today.

And they have defeated him by the blood of the Lamb and by their testimony. And they did not love their lives so much that they were afraid to die.

REVELATION 12:11

Prayer Prompt

Lord, I will use my voice! Show me how to overcome by using my testimony . . .

If Not Now, When?

Janna had been nursing a dream of owning her own business for as long as she could remember. She'd spent months writing her business plan after years of research. She knew her competitors and industry statistics like she knew her own name. Yet something was holding her back. Janna kept putting off her launch: "I'll launch when I get another degree." "I'll share it once my audience is larger." "I need a big name to attract people to this idea."

Her list of excuses made it impossible for Janna to actually do what she'd planned. Her excuses were keeping her away from her assignment. I eventually asked her, "If not now, then when?" Because we do not know how much time we have here on earth, it is imperative that we carry out our call daily. We cannot wait on the perfect timing. Instead we are called to be obedient and press on (Phil. 3:14).

I had my own "If not now, then when?" moment years ago with my first women's ministry conference, Exhale. It wasn't perfect, with all of the lighting, design, and technical wonder. Instead it was a dimly lit gathering in the back of the facility we were renting for church. If I hadn't taken that step, I likely wouldn't be leading thousands of women around the globe through the Permission experience now.

God is pressing us in this season. It's time to GO! If not

now, when? When are you going to face that fear? When are you going to move past your doubt? When are you going to step up and be who God has called you to be? *Now* is always a good time to follow God. Don't delay your future any longer. The time is now!

What is one thing that you have been putting off? What action will you take today to be ready when the time comes?

Why, you do not even know what will happen tomorrow. What is your life? You are a mist that appears for a little while and then vanishes.

JAMES 4:14 (NIV)

Prayer Prompt

Lord, the time is now! I choose to stop delaying and press towards what You have for me . . .

Pray with Expectation

Have you ever noticed how children don't hesitate to ask for things? From small snacks to promising toys on television, they make their requests known. Not only that, they expect to receive what they ask for! My sons are like that—especially for birthdays and Christmas. They know that something they have asked for will be among their gifts when the time comes. Unfortunately, many of us have lost that childlike boldness. We have lost the hope and confidence that leads to expectation.

As daughters of the King, we have explicit permission. We have permission to ask. More important, we can expect a response (Matt. 7:7–8). God is not like earthly fathers who have limits and budgets. He doesn't break promises. He doesn't ignore us. He responds. We must pray with expectation that He will respond to our request in one way or another. What I love about our permission to pray with expectation is that our expectations aren't just limited to tangible things. We often live without wisdom, peace, and joy—the intangibles. All simply because we don't pray with expectation. Sis, we can pray with the expectation that He can provide this for us too.

I want to remind you today that you do not pray in vain! We serve a God who answers prayers! From the biggest to the smallest thing in your life, God is concerned about it. Trust the Lord to lead you as you pray. Prayer has changed my whole life in *every way*, and I know it will change yours. He is your Father. Ask of Him what you desire.

Think back to when you lost hope and confidence in expectation of a good outcome. Ask the Lord to repair the broken place of doubt.

And if we know that he hears us—whatever we ask—we know that we have what we asked of him.

1 JOHN 5:15 (NIV)

Prayer Prompt

Thank You, Lord, for answering my prayers.
Guide me and lead me as I pray . . .

It's Worth The Wait

In generations past the characters of Big Mama and Madea would start their Sunday dinners the night before. There were no microwaves either, so though the meals were ready, there was often an additional wait after church while the dishes were reheated. After their love and labor, the meals were delicious and filling. I believe that something happened when the food was left to cool down and simmer in its juices and seasonings overnight. Whatever it was, the meals they prepared were always good and most certainly worth the wait.

I loved how families and communities came together to enjoy those meals. No interruptions. No rushing. Just enjoyment of the moment, with the matriarch looking on with pride and joy as her family savored what she'd worked to put together. God is preparing things for us too. He's stirring in love while anticipating our fullness. But we have to be patient. We are instructed to wait on Him (Ps. 27:14). We are also given specific rewards for waiting, including renewed strength and endurance (Isa. 40:31). I can use more of both!

Listen to me: What God has for you is worth the wait! Don't cheat the process. You want to wait on His goodness. Don't allow yourself to settle for only a piece of the promise. God desires for you to experience the fullness of what He has for you! Any day you consider making it happen on your own, remind yourself that God is faithful to do what He promised (Ps. 145:13), and His Word is worth waiting on!

What have you been rushing to manifest in your life in this season? Remain in good courage while waiting. Expect a beautiful outcome.

Let us hold fast the confession of our hope without wavering, for he who promised is faithful.

HEBREWS 10:23 (ESV)

Prayer Prompt

Father, I will wait on You! I believe that I will see the fullness of what You've promised . . .

Don't Lose Faith

The last few days of our devotional time have been focused on expecting and waiting. But if I can be honest, there have been times when the expectation and the wait felt overwhelming for me. In those moments I've been tempted to lose faith, to give up. I just want to move on to the next thing, because the thing I'm sitting with is just taking too long to get to me. Sound familiar?

I love that we serve a faithful God who is there for us even when we want to give up. He's there reminding us that His strength is made perfect in our weakness (2 Cor. 12:9). We serve a loving Father who is reminding us to have faith. Remember He told us it's impossible to please Him without faith (Heb. 11:6)? That means we can't lose it now. We've come this far by faith, as the old church used to say. But I like to add a little Dr. Jackie on it: "It ain't over till it's good!" This statement recognizes that if we haven't made it to good, then it can't be over. So don't lose faith!

That situation you want to be over—the one that seems *impossible* to fix? God can fix it in the blink of an eye. The fact that He hasn't means there's something He wants to birth through that situation. Don't lose faith because it's hard. In those hard times remember that we serve an extraordinary God who uses situations, just like the one you're in *right now*, to make you extraordinary too! It's not up to us to fix the thing in our own strength. It's not up to us to figure it out. We are commanded to continue to do the good work.

What good works have you contemplated giving up because the outcome isn't coming as soon as you want it to?

So let's not get tired of doing what is good. At just the right time we will reap a harvest of blessing if we don't give up.

GALATIANS 6:9

Prayer Prompt

Thank You, Lord, for giving me the strength to endure! I won't give up on the call on my life . . .

It's Time to Push

This journey of remaining in love has involved a lot of waiting. A lot of patience. A lot of faith. Anytime God calls me to a new season or assignment, I think about pregnancy. Each of my pregnancies was different, from how I carried to what I craved. One child was super chill in the womb. Another son couldn't help dancing as soon as I got still for the night. Our other boy was a roller coaster of movement followed by stillness—just like he is now. But there were a few consistent elements in all three pregnancies. God's timing on my sons' arrivals was perfect and intentional. There were discomforts. There were fears. There were challenges, especially with my firstborn's early arrival. Bed rest. Diet changes. Habit adjustments. Carrying life each time required significant lifestyle adaptations. Not making the right decisions could have resulted in very different outcomes for all of us. I trusted God to lead. He trusted me to obey.

There have been some things that God has entrusted each of us with that have been growing inside of us. We have been tasked with carrying them through the process of gestation. It may be a business idea. It could be a strategy for helping your family eliminate generational cycles. He may have trusted you to steward a new product or process in the world. You've been praying for it. You've been preparing for it. It's time for the promise to be delivered.

Our God is a God of miracles! He will always exceed our natural abilities. Listen to me—it's time to push! Push past your limitations, push past your fears, and get ready to birth what God has for you!

Has God made you a promise but you've accepted the limitations that keep you from getting to that promise? The appointed time for the vision is now, and it will not fail.

For the vision is yet for the appointed time;
It hastens toward the goal and it will
not fail.
Though it tarries, wait for it;
For it will certainly come, it will not
delay.

HABAKKUK 2:3 (NASB)

Prayer Prompt

Lord, I'm ready to push! Exceed my natural abilities and push me towards Your promise . . .

There's More

After losing everything in a fire, Linda was taken aback when her friend and coworker suggested they tell others in the office what was going on in Linda's life. She almost let her embarrassment, shame, and pride push aside the truth—she was in dire need of basic necessities. Her department head called her into a mandatory meeting in the conference room where her coworkers were gathered. As she looked around, there were stacks of things she needed. Toiletries. Household basics. Cleaning supplies. Towels. Clothes. Kitchen appliances. And even a few decorative items like picture frames and filled flower vases. Linda began to weep at the sight of all of the things gathered, overwhelmed by the generosity of her peers, some of whom she'd never met. While making plans to get everything to her new place, a former supervisor said, "Wait, there's more. We need your Zelle to send over the cash for things that aren't here."

When we are facing challenges and lack, I imagine the Father stepping in right on time with a blessing. And then I hear Him saying, "But wait, there's more." When we trust Him with our situations, His Word assures us that He will do above and beyond what we can ask, think, or imagine (Eph. 3:20). Now I don't know about you, but I can get in a place of thinking big and believing bigger for how He's going to work something out. And every single time He still finds a way to blow my mind with more!

This season of love is about abundance. It's about the more. God wants you to have more! After everything you've been through, His blessing contains more. Concerning your life, God says "More." *There is more for you!*

Lay your worrisome situation on the altar today. Trust God to handle it with more.

There's more to come: We continue to shout our praise even when we're hemmed in with troubles, because we know how troubles can develop passionate patience in us.

ROMANS 5:3 (MSG)

Prayer Prompt

Lord, help me to stay alert to whatever You will do next. I believe there is more for me . . .

No Obligation

Recently I came across this post that said, "We don't know what we like; we like what we know." And it made me pause. How many things have I said that I liked because that's just what I know? I used a certain laundry detergent brand because that's what my mother used. I used a specific hair care product because that's what my college roommate always used. I continued to use those products because they were what I knew, not because they were necessarily the best for the task at hand.

I think about this concept when it comes to our behaviors. How many times do we feel obligated to stay in a dysfunctional relationship because that's what we saw growing up? How common is it for us to pop off at the mouth when something doesn't go our way because that's what we've always done? What obligation do we have to habits that we learned for survival that no longer serve the place in life we are in? We don't have an obligation to those behaviors. We don't have obligations to the people we were before accepting our role as beloved daughters.

In this new season you have no obligation to your old life habits. You have absolutely no obligation to obey your flesh or what it's urging you to do. The Spirit of God that raised Jesus from the dead lives in you! That Spirit was powerful enough to make the impossible more than a possibility. God is giving you life through that same Spirit. Command your flesh to obey the Lord!

What patterns, habits, and behaviors is God urging you to release in this season?

———

Therefore, dear brothers and sisters, you have no obligation to do what your sinful nature urges you to do.
ROMANS 8:12

Prayer Prompt

Daddy, thank You for giving me authority
over my flesh. No more obligation to
living the way I used to live . . .

Give Generously

Growing up in the '80s, no one wanted to be the stingy one; it was an insult. We all wanted to appear like we had it all together, with more than enough to go around. Though there were times we really didn't have anything to give, the offense of being perceived as stingy or not having enough was greater. I think about those times with the gifts and resources God has given us now, and I'm not just talking about monetary gifts. Many of us have other gifts, including time and talent. Whatever the resource, we should always give generously.

In most cases, God has given us so much more than we can handle. It's part of the abundant life He's promised us. To be lenders and not borrowers. Yet sometimes those old habits of lack and feelings of fear keep us from sharing. We hide our gifts. We keep our blessings to ourselves because we don't want anyone to ask for anything. And then there are some of us who are ashamed of having more. We don't want people to make the assumption that we're stuck-up because we have certain access and resources. So we play it down. That's not the way we are supposed to live.

The Bible says that the godly give generously! Allow that to be your heart posture day to day. God has given to us generously, so we should give to others with that same measure! Every time you pour out love, pour it out generously. Every time you pour out faith, pour it out generously. Whenever you've been in need, you didn't want just a little—you wanted a generous gift! Be what you need today. Respond generously!

In what areas can you become a more generous giver?

———

The wicked borrow and never repay, but the godly are generous givers.

PSALM 37:21

—— *Prayer Prompt* ——

Lord, I want to be like You! Teach me
how to be a generous giver . . .

Fix Your Focus

It's been said that driving windows—the front windshields of cars—are bigger than the back windows and rearview mirrors because we are supposed to keep our focus on the road ahead more than what's behind. I like to add that this is also why the side mirrors are small. These smaller mirrors are not our primary focus when navigating to our destinations. When driving, the most important thing is right in front of us, the road ahead. The lanes beside us and traffic behind us are not to command our full attention. They are reference points. They let us know how far we've come. They tell us what's coming up beside us if we need to change lanes. But the main priority is looking where we're going and driving forward. The same holds true with our focus on our assignments. We are charged to stay the course, not turning or swerving to the right or left (Prov. 4:27).

As daughters of Christ, we must learn to fix our eyes on the Lord. God is always calling us to look at Him! Don't look at people, your circumstances, or even yourself. Fix your focus on the one who is able to comfort you. The more you focus on God, the bigger He becomes, and your issues will become smaller and smaller. Check your focus today!

Name an area where you've allowed the focus to become bigger than God. Repent and ask the Lord for redirection.

———

. . . fixing our eyes on Jesus, the pioneer and perfecter of faith. For the joy set before him he endured the cross, scorning its shame, and sat down at the right hand of the throne of God.

HEBREWS 12:2–3 (NIV)

Prayer Prompt

Father, I will fix my eyes on You! Thank
You for redirecting my focus . . .

Check Your Thoughts

I walked into a classroom with walls covered by inspirational posters. One read, "Watch your thoughts, they become your words; watch your words, they become your actions; watch your actions, they become your habits; watch your habits, they become your character; watch your character, it becomes your destiny (Lao Tzu)."

The poster was a reminder that what we thought would ultimately influence what we became. I saw it happen on more than one occasion. My classmates were convinced they didn't have what it would take to move on to the next level. Sure enough, when the time came, they'd be stuck with their lives playing out exactly the way they thought and confessed they would. Early in life I didn't understand this quote in its fullness. However, as an adult I can see exactly how it unfolds in our lives, time and time again. As a believer, I understand how so many scriptures were dedicated to the meditations of our heart, the things we think about constantly. There are over one hundred scriptures about guarding our heart. God is trying to get our attention in this area.

Your thoughts control your actions. Your actions become associated with your character. What have you been thinking about? What has come to be in your life as a result of your thoughts? My mentor, author Dr. Anita Phillips, explains it this way: Negative thoughts are able to take root and dominate because of the condition of our hearts. Therefore, if we want to sustain a better thought life, we need to give attention to our heart.[5]

Dear sister, your past and current situations do not dictate what God says about you. It's time to check your thoughts and bring them into alignment with the Word and the will of the Father. Choose today to have God-thoughts that will produce God-actions.

Interrogate and disallow the activity of certain thoughts that are currently running rampant in your mind. Make a list of what God's words say instead.

We demolish arguments and every pretension that sets itself up against the knowledge of God, and we take captive every thought to make it obedient to Christ.

2 CORINTHIANS 10:5 (NIV)

Prayer Prompt

Daddy, I choose today to take authority over every thought that goes against what You say about me . . .

Go and Do the Same

I go hard for my sisters and daughters in the Permission Room. Hard in prayer. Deep in questions at the Permission Talk Table. Open in how I share. And I do it because someone did it for me. First there was Christ, who made the decision long before my time on earth began that I was worth saving. He left this world and continues to intercede on my behalf to this day. Then there are the women who've come into covenant with me over the years. Family. Friends. They've made sure that I feel the love of God in a tangible way. When I am down, they minister to me. When I am succeeding, they praise God with me. As He pours into me through them, I feel joy and a calling to do the same for others. The Permission Room, Forward City Church, and other platforms give me an opportunity to go and do the same—spread love.

Aren't you grateful for the love of Jesus? He's lifted us from low places and touched us where we were! His love is unconditional, never-ending, and relentless! He doesn't abandon us in the hard places. He doesn't shun us in the dark places. His love is unchanging in every season. In the same way that the Father has loved us, He challenges us to go and do the same. Take that love that God has shown you, and show it to someone else!

What mercy and favor has the Lord shown you?

How can you share love with someone else today?

And he said, "He who showed mercy on him." Then Jesus said to him, "Go and do likewise."

LUKE 10:37 (NKJV)

Prayer Prompt

Lord, thank You for Your love! Show me how to love people in the same way that You've loved me . . .

Be Grateful

Speaker and bestselling author Valorie Burton often shares how gratitude is a characteristic of successful women. She explains, "Gratitude is powerful. It keeps you from taking things for granted."[6] What she and other leading women—including Joyce Meyer—have identified is the connection between gratitude and our overall well-being. We feel better and do better when we are thankful. You may have noticed it too. If I'm having a bad moment, I pause and think about what I'm grateful for. *This could be worse. The blessing in this is . . . I'm so grateful that this moment cannot last forever.* My attitude makes a huge difference in the perspective on my situation. When I choose gratitude, I see how much bigger God is than my current situation, discomfort, or inconvenience. Choosing gratitude even when I'm still waiting for an outcome delivers joy faster than simply waiting in misery.

If you look back over your life and begin to think about the faithfulness of God, you'll have no choice but to be full of gratitude. If you're reading this, *you're still here*! The fact that you're still here is proof that the enemy lost. Let gratefulness overwhelm you today—it will be your strength to keep going.

Make a gratitude list of the victories you've

won with the Lord on your side.

But thanks be to God, who gives us the victory through
our Lord Jesus Christ.

1 CORINTHIANS 15:57 (NKJV)

Prayer Prompt

Lord, thank You for being so faithful
after all these years! Teach me how to
live with a heart of gratitude . . .

Say Thank You

During a recent conversation on nagging, my husband pointed out that gratitude can soften a request for improvement. Think about the differences between these two phrases: "I know you see this trash running over" versus "It's really helpful when you take the trash out." Which do you think my husband is more likely to respond to? The one that's got a bit of gratitude and appreciation on it. And when that gratitude is shared frequently, he's more likely to continue serving well.

Similarly, if our relationship is anchored in expressing thankfulness for the things that are going well, when the moments of feedback come, they're received better. I don't take a suggestion as an attack when I know that my spouse is appreciative in general. And I also know that once I implement the feedback or make a concerted effort towards improvement, Travis is going to acknowledge it with "I appreciate you doing . . ."

In marriage and other relationships, it's easy to have unspoken expectations and take the other person's participation for granted. However, when we add a genuine thank-you, we're likely to experience a better relationship. It's the same in our relationship with the Father. We become so comfortable with His position as **El Shaddai—God Almighty, the All-Sufficient One**—that we forget to say thank you. We find ourselves caught up in an "Oh, God is going to take care of that" mindset because

He has always been all the things and is capable of everything. But I don't want us to take Him for granted like we do our other relationships. We have to say thank you.

How many times has God healed you or come through for you? What situations has He turned around for your benefit? We would not be where we are today without His grace. He has been *faithful*! I pray that the Lord never lets us forget all the many ways He has made for us! We shall be the ones to come back and say thank you!

Take five minutes and call someone and share what you are most grateful for in your life right now. You will be amazed at how contagious gratitude is.

One of them, when he saw he was healed, came back, praising God in a loud voice. He threw himself at Jesus' feet and thanked him—and he was a Samaritan.

LUKE 17:15–16 (NIV)

Prayer Prompt

Daddy, thank You for all You've done! Teach me how to live with a heart of gratitude . . .

Give Your Best

Our three children are very different from each other in their demeanors and personalities. We realized this early on when each of them was born. Although they're our sons, with the same parents, their ways of being could not be more different. Our oldest son is more like his mommy. He is very relational; he cares deeply about his connection with others. Our middle son is just like his dad in every way. He is so creative and advanced. And our baby boy is in a league of his own. He marches to the beat of his own drum. Their differences become clearer with them being in school. The three of them process and excel differently. One of the things we've been diligent about is reminding them to do their best. We realize that what's the best for one may not be the best for another.

God grants us this same grace when we give to Him. He instructs us to give according to what we have, not in competition with the person next to us or someone on the internet. We also are not called to give God just anything. The story of Cain and Abel illustrates this clearly. Cain brought some of his fruit as an offering. Abel brought his best portions as an offering. The Lord had favor on Abel's offering and no regard for Cain's (Gen. 4:3–5).

Sometimes we have a strong misconception that it's good enough to just give. But God is requiring more of us! As He is asking you to give whatever facet of yourself, which could be giving your time or talent or resources, check yourself: Are you just giving *some* or are you giving *your best*? Don't just think about *what* you do, but *how* you do it. We must give what is particular, or specific, to who we are. Our giving is in connection to how God made us.

Everybody can give God something, but we want to be children of God who give Him our personal best!

Whatever you do [whatever your task may be], work from the soul [that is, put in your very best effort], as [something done] for the Lord and not for men.

COLOSSIANS 3:23 (AMP)

Prayer Prompt

Lord, I give my absolute best to You! I give You the best of my time, talents, and resources . . .

Don't Settle

I believe that there is a difference between good and great. I even asked my husband about this sentiment during a recent podcast. I wanted my audience, largely women, to hear from a man about how men know the difference between a "simple good" thing and a "God's good" thing when it comes to choosing a spouse. In addition to marriage, there are so many other good opportunities that come to us. But we have to have discernment as to whether it's simply a good thing or a God thing. What makes a good thing great is when it's a God thing. When we choose good over God, no matter how good it is, it's still settling. Settling is suboptimal. It is showing up beneath the will of God.

God's way should always be our goal, and it always leads to an abundant life. Our ability to yield opens us and makes us better at touching and blessing people the way God specifically wants. You are a daughter of God—you don't have to settle in any area of your life. Truthfully, there is absolutely no reason for you to settle! Be willing to wait on what God has for you. His plan is perfect! I just want to remind you that what God has for you isn't just good—it's the *best* thing for you. It's a *God thing*. Step out there and trust what God is saying concerning your life. Don't settle; go after the great thing, the God thing.

Ask God to reveal the areas in which you have settled. Trust Him to rework the situation.

The Spirit of God whets our appetite by giving us a taste of what's ahead. He puts a little of heaven in our hearts so that we'll never settle for less.

2 CORINTHIANS 5:5 (MSG)

Prayer Prompt

God, thank You for Your perfect plan
for my life. Teach me how to not settle
in this new season of my life . . .

In His Image

My assistant has been with me for so long that she can often tell what I'm thinking before I even say anything. She often anticipates my response to a situation and eliminates hindrances that would keep me from operating at my best. The more time we spend with a person, the more likely we are to understand their mannerisms. Over time we may even begin to adopt some of their behaviors as our own. I see it all the time with best friends and couples. They start to look, sound, and even act alike.

The same is true when we spend intimate time with the Father. We begin to take on more of His image. We start to sound like Him—speaking life. We begin to look like Him—shining radiantly when we show up. We begin to act like Him—extending love to all we encounter. Getting to that place requires time and attention. Operating in His image requires intention, vulnerability, and intimacy. And reflecting His image is the next level the Father is calling us to.

One of the greatest compliments a father can receive is that their child looks, acts, and sounds like them. And this is a compliment that never grows old. As our children become older, we always expect them to emulate us more and more. Our heavenly Father is the exact same way. He is always after us being more and more like Him. We have to continually give Him a yes for that godly shaping to continue. He will always require more of us!

What has God been pressing you to do lately? Does He want you to get up earlier? Fast more? All of this is producing a new level in you. Trust Him—it's necessary to reflect His image!

What part of God's image are you expecting to emulate in this season? Ask for the steps to make it so.

So all of us who have had that veil removed can see and reflect the glory of the Lord. And the Lord—who is the Spirit—makes us more and more like him as we are changed into his glorious image.

2 CORINTHIANS 3:18

Prayer Prompt

Lord, show me the next level You have for me.
I surrender to becoming more like You . . .

Speak Life

In early psychology courses, professors introduce a concept called "self-fulfilling prophecy." The *Encyclopedia Britannica* defines "self-fulfilling prophecy" as the "process through which an originally false expectation leads to its own confirmation."[7] Simply put, we can keep predicting or speaking an outcome until it becomes true. I think about how God handled Zechariah in the book of Luke. God was planning to do a magnificent work through Zechariah's wife, Elizabeth. But Zechariah had a little sarcasm in his response to the angel. Instead of allowing Zechariah's mouth to negate the promise, the Lord made him mute until the word came to pass. Imagine if God rendered us unable to speak every time we spoke something contrary to His Word or plans! Our words carry with them life and death. It is up to us to choose life. To agree with what God has spoken. To affirm His promises. We are called to speak life.

Your words of encouragement can be life-changing to those around you. Always give life with the words you speak! So often we're quick to call out negative things in the people that we're closest to, like our spouse, our children, or our friends. Let's challenge ourselves to be even quicker to celebrate, encourage, and affirm them in the Lord!

Put yourself on a life-speaking fast. For the next three days refuse to speak anything negative. Only speak what is good and beneficial to the building of yourself and others. Speak life.

The tongue can bring death or life;
those who love to talk will reap the
consequences.

PROVERBS 18:21

Prayer Prompt

Father, I want my words to give life! Help me to speak
words of encouragement to those around me . . .

Shine Your Light

Eileen was comfortable in the background. In fact, she hated having the spotlight on her. She served well in administration and did well supporting others behind the scenes, but she also began to feel a tug to do more. At work she was encouraged to take on more leadership roles, eventually landing her an executive-level position. Eileen noticed the same thing happening in church. Each time she tried to hide, she ended up in the front—leading the choir, directing the dancers, heading up the media team. For all the years she'd been hiding in the background, God was calling her into His marvelous light. He'd attached a call to her obedience to step forward. As a result, more people were drawn to Him through her. Eileen had a particular style and approach that allowed others to feel the love of God through her demeanor. She didn't have to change who she was. Her authenticity in the light of God's love was just what others needed to see as an example.

To do the tasks God has called us, we have to be who He has called us to be. And to be that person, we must remain in His light! When we dim our light, we lose the ability to properly see ourselves and others lose the ability to see us. Without light we live powerless, because lack of light means lack of God. Choose not to live in lack when He's called you to abundant life. Refuse to be hidden in this season. Push back against the desire to remain in darkness. Shine the light He gave you!

Confront the area in which you have been hiding your light. Identify why this has been your choice and how you will shine moving forward.

You are the light of the world—like a city on a hilltop that cannot be hidden.

MATTHEW 5:14

Prayer Prompt

God, I want to shine the light You've given me! Give me the power that comes from living in the light . . .

Keep Leading Me

Living with a singer/songwriter means that I regularly consume a lot of music. Even if nothing is playing, something is being hummed. During a recent interview I was asked about my favorite song. It was hard to decide because I have so many favorites! So I took a deep breath and answered honestly.

I don't have a favorite song so much as a sticking refrain right now. The group Tribl hosted a live recording and worship night at Forward City. They did a little tag to a song, and it has become the theme of my life right now. "Keep leading me," it repeats a few times over. I keep listening to it and being encouraged. He's leading me. It reminds me that God is not just a shepherd but a good shepherd. That's the theme of my life in this particular season: He's a good father, a good shepherd.

My husband often says that we have the choice to live guided or guessing. I think we often settle for a life of guessing because we don't recognize that our Lord, who is all-powerful, also desires to be **Adonai—Lord and Master** in our day-to-day. "Keep leading me" reminds me of this truth and helps me remember that He desires to be close to me. It speaks of the intimacy found as I walk in step with the Lord.

As your shepherd, God desires to lead and guide you through *everything*! No matter how big or small an experience is, you are not meant to wander through life. Either you're living guided or you're living guessing! Don't get ahead of Him and don't get too far behind Him. Allow Him to guide you step-by-step into whatever He has for you next!

Spend time inviting the Father to keep leading you in your efforts throughout the day.

The LORD is my shepherd; I shall not want.
PSALM 23:1 (KJV)

Prayer Prompt

Lord, thank You for leading me. I surrender to You so that You can guide me through life . . .

Remain in Love

Relationships are commitments. They require us to do the work necessary to continue in healthy unity. There may be days that you don't like a certain person. There will also be days that you completely disagree with those close to you. However, remaining in love is a choice followed by intentional action. We choose to love a person. We choose to remain in relationship with them. We choose to do things to foster feelings of love. And when we do, beautiful things are produced. Marriages. Families. Communities. Partnerships.

The same holds true for our relationship with our heavenly Father. When we remain in Him, fruit is produced. We respond to our calls and assignments affirmatively. We accept our reflection as the image of Him. We walk with courage and confidence. We choose great over good. Our thoughts and habits align with God's will. Our lights shine in the earth. When we remain in love, we bear good fruit. Our consistent time in His presence is an expression of how we remain in love with our Father and how He remains in love with us. Remain in love.

What practices and habits will you incorporate in your life to remain in love?

Remain in me, and I will remain in you. For a branch cannot produce fruit if it is severed from the vine, and you cannot be fruitful unless you remain in me.

JOHN 15:4

Prayer Prompt

Daddy, I cannot be fruitful without You.
Help me to remain in Your love . . .

Remaining in His Love

Every relationship takes work. Good relationships take both effort and commitment. As you consider your role in building intimacy with God, highlight the areas in which you're excelling. Take time to identify opportunities for growth. Remember, your relationship with Him requires honesty and vulnerability. You have to do the work to see the results.

- Ways I'm pursuing a deeper relationship with the Lord . . .
- Areas I can grow and improve when it comes to my relationship with the Father . . .
- One way that I can remain in love with God . . .
- One way that I can lead with love in my life . . .

Conclusion

REFLECT AND REMAIN

Sis, when I closed my first book, *Permission to Live Free*, with thoughts on being beloved, I had no idea God would lead me to extend that charge to this level. What a journey this has been! And I love that it continues. It continues with us seeking the Father. It continues with us basking in His love for us. I'm so honored that He would choose us to be in relationship with. From reminding us of our status as beloved daughters to bombarding us with His promises concerning our purpose to giving us permission to live freely, His love for us is evident. On the permission journey we can choose to live loved. When we are rooted in God's love for us, we're secure. We are loved.

Though the 90 days have come to an end, our relationship with the Lord continues. We must continue to pursue Him with the same fervor and persistence. I hope you're ready to finish what you've started! What are the things that you have come to hold on to in your intimate time with Him? What are some ways that you will remain in love as you move forward?

I pray that from now on, when you are seeking clarity in any area of life, that you find it in the fullness of His love. That you remain in His love as you are and as you will become. There's such a freedom that exists when we tap into our permission, authenticity, and obedience. There's freedom in His love. Sis, that's real life. The one God created for you. For me. For us. A life remaining in love.

With love,

Dr. Jackie

Let's pray together.

God, thank You for loving me. I'm humbled and honored to be transformed by Your love. You have proven that I am Your beloved daughter time and again. You have confirmed that my identity and purpose flourish under the nourishment of Your love. And I'm so grateful. Thank You, Father, for counting me as worthy. Thank You for loving me simply because I am Yours. I choose to remain in love with You. I'm so grateful that I fell in love. For, Daddy, You are love! I will remain here, in Jesus' name, amen.

Affirmed in Love

I mentioned in the day 90 devotion that remaining in love is a choice. In addition to time and conversation, sometimes we just need a reminder of who the other person is and who we are. We find comfort in remembering the things that drew us to a person.

We also benefit from glimpses of ourselves through the eyes of others. Maybe they admire our beauty in a way we've never considered. Or they acknowledge aspects of our intellect that have rarely been appreciated. Or they view our preferences as endearing instead of nuisances. As a result, we see ourselves through additional lenses of love.

Then there are those times where we have to take deliberate authority over our thoughts and actions. We question whether a habit is more annoying than quirky. We tell ourselves something needs to change for us to be loved and accepted. Or we simply have a moment of self-doubt that causes us to question everything. That's what this section is for—*all those things*—quick references and reminders of who the Father is, who we are, and what His promises are toward us. When you want to affirm what is most true about God's demonstrations of love, use these scriptures to build your faith.

GOD IS LOVE

AFFIRMATION	SCRIPTURES
My heavenly Father is a promise keeper.	Joshua 23:14 Psalm 145:13 Romans 4:21 2 Corinthians 1:20
My Father is a healer.	Psalm 147:3 Jeremiah 30:17 Mark 5:34 Acts 9:34
God is my source and provider.	Genesis 22:8 Psalm 145:16 Ezekiel 34:26 Luke 12:24
The Lord is attentive to me.	1 Kings 9:3 Psalm 23:1 Isaiah 65:24 Jeremiah 29:12
God operates in abundance.	John 10:10 2 Corinthians 9:8 Ephesians 2:4 Philippians 4:19

God is trustworthy.	Psalm 111:7 Isaiah 26:4 Lamentations 3:22 Ezekiel 37:14
The Father gives me peace.	Isaiah 26:3 Romans 15:13 Colossians 3:15 2 Thessalonians 3:16
God is always with me.	Genesis 28:13 1 Chronicles 28:20 Psalm 16:8 Isaiah 41:10
The Lord fights for me.	Exodus 14:14 Deuteronomy 3:22 Joshua 23:10 Psalm 109:21
God the Father is loving.	Psalm 36:7 Psalm 86:15 Zephaniah 3:17 1 John 3:1

I AM HIS BELOVED DAUGHTER

AFFIRMATION	SCRIPTURES
I am the daughter of Abba Father.	Psalm 45:13 Psalm 144:12 Proverbs 31:25 2 Corinthians 6:18
I matter to the Father.	Numbers 6:24–26 Psalm 8:4–6 Psalm 139:17 Romans 5:8
I was created for a purpose.	Proverbs 16:4 Ecclesiastes 3:1 Ephesians 1:11 Ephesians 2:10
I have authority through the Father.	Genesis 1:28 Matthew 16:19 Luke 10:19 Ephesians 3:12
I am a joint heir with Jesus Christ.	Galatians 3:29 Galatians 4:7 Ephesians 3:6 Titus 3:7

Father God is responsive to my cries.	Jeremiah 33:3 Luke 11:9 John 16:24 Philippians 4:6
I am made in the image of a good father.	Genesis 1:27 Romans 8:29 Ephesians 4:24 Colossians 3:10
God had plans for me before I was born.	Psalm 139:16 Isaiah 44:2 Jeremiah 1:5 Jeremiah 29:11
I am seen and chosen.	Psalm 129:1 John 15:16 Ephesians 1:4 1 Peter 2:9
I am made whole and well.	Mark 10:52 1 Thessalonians 5:223 1 Peter 5:10 3 John 1:2

God's Promises When You . . .

Feel Guilty
Psalm 130:3–4
Romans 8:1–2
1 Corinthians 6:11
Ephesians 3:12
Hebrews 10:22–23

Feel Dejected
Psalm 130:7
Isaiah 65:24
Matthew 11:28–30
Romans 8:26–27
Hebrews 4:16
James 4:8, 10

Feel Despair
Psalm 119:116
Isaiah 57:15
Jeremiah 32:17
Philippians 4:6–7

Feel Disappointment
Psalm 22:4–5
Matthew 19:25–26

John 15:7
Romans 8:28
Ephesians 3:20
James 1:5–6

Feel Depressed
Deuteronomy 31:8
Psalm 34:18
Isaiah 49:13–15
Romans 5:5

Feel Anxious
Psalm 55:22
Isaiah 41:13
Matthew 6:24–25
Matthew 11:28–29
Philippians 4:6–7
1 Peter 5:7

Feel Impatient
Psalm 27:13–14
Psalm 37:7, 9
Romans 2:7
1 Timothy 1:16

Hebrews 6:12
2 Peter 3:9

Feel Confused
Psalm 32:8
Isaiah 42:16
John 8:12
John 14:27
1 Corinthians 2:15–16
James 1:5

Feel Weak
Psalm 72:13
Isaiah 41:10
Romans 8:26
1 Corinthians 1:7–9
2 Corinthians 4:7–9
2 Corinthians 12:9–10

Feel Afraid
Joshua 1:9
Psalm 4:8
Psalm 23:4
Romans 8:37–39
2 Corinthians 1:10
2 Timothy 1:7
Hebrews 13:6

Grieve
Psalm 119:50, 76–77
Jeremiah 31:13
Matthew 5:4
John 16:20–22
1 Thessalonians 4:13–14
Revelation 21:3–4

Suffer
Psalm 34:19
Nahum 1:7
John 16:33
Romans 8:16–17
1 Peter 2:20–21
1 Peter 4:12–13

Fail
Joshua 1:9
Romans 3:23–24
Romans 5:8
Hebrews 10:35–36
1 John 1:8–9

Doubt
Psalm 34:22
Matthew 14:28–33
John 3:18
James 1:5–8
Hebrews 11:1, 6

Bible Reading Plan

Of all the reasons people mention for not reading the Bible, simple discouragement is the most common. The Bible's length alone is imposing. More like a self-contained library than a book, it includes sixty-six different books by several dozen authors. No wonder people get confused and discouraged.

The following reading plan helps break these books of the Bible into more manageable portions, assigning about one chapter a day, which should take only five to ten minutes to read.

Introduction to the New Testament

Time Commitment: One month
Goal: Survey New Testament biblical foundations

This is a great place to start reading the Bible. Two separate reading plans take you quickly into passages of the New Testament every Christian should know. These were selected with two concerns in mind: First, the passages are frequently quoted or referred to. Second, they are relatively easy to read and understand.

Two Weeks on the Life and Teachings of Jesus

- [ ] 1 **Luke 1:** Preparing for His Arrival
- [ ] 2 **Luke 2:** Story of His Birth
- [ ] 3 **Mark 1:** Beginning of His Ministry
- [ ] 4 **Mark 9:** Day in His Life
- [ ] 5 **Matthew 5:** Sermon on the Mount
- [ ] 6 **Matthew 6:** Sermon on the Mount
- [ ] 7 **Luke 15:** Parables of Jesus
- [ ] 8 **John 3:** Conversation with Nicodemus
- [ ] 9 **John 14:** His Final Instructions
- [ ] 10 **John 17:** Prayer for His Disciples
- [ ] 11 **Matthew 26:** His Betrayal and Arrest
- [ ] 12 **Matthew 27:** Execution on a Cross
- [ ] 13 **John 20:** Jesus' Resurrection
- [ ] 14 **Luke 24:** Appearances After the Resurrection

Two Weeks on the Life and Teachings of Paul

- [ ] 1 **Acts 9:** Conversion
- [ ] 2 **Acts 16:** Macedonian Call and Jailbreak
- [ ] 3 **Acts 17:** Missionary Journeys
- [ ] 4 **Acts 26:** Life Story
- [ ] 5 **Acts 27:** Shipwreck
- [ ] 6 **Acts 28:** Arrival in Rome
- [ ] 7 **Romans 3:** Theology Summary
- [ ] 8 **Romans 7:** Struggle with Sin
- [ ] 9 **Romans 8:** Life in the Spirit
- [ ] 10 **1 Corinthians 13:** Description of Love
- [ ] 11 **1 Corinthians 15:** Thoughts on the Afterlife
- [ ] 12 **Galatians 5:** Freedom in Christ
- [ ] 13 **Ephesians 3:** Summary of Mission
- [ ] 14 **Philippians 2:** Imitating Christ

Prayers in the Psalms

The Psalms include many prayers. We've grouped them together by theme to help you find inspiration and comfort no matter your circumstances.

THEME	CHAPTERS IN THE PSALMS
Morning Prayer	5
Evening Prayer	4
Thanksgiving	65, 111, 136
Praise and Worship	24, 67, 92, 100, 113, 150
Trusting God	37, 62
Longing for God	27, 42, 63, 84
When We Need Guidance	25
When We Need Deliverance	40, 116
When We Need Forgiveness	51, 130
God as Our Shepherd	23
God's Help in Trouble	66, 69, 86, 102, 140, 143
God's Constant Love and Care	89, 103, 107, 146
God's Majesty and Glory	8, 29, 93, 104
God's Knowledge and Presence	139
God's Word, the Bible	19, 119
God's Protection	46, 91, 125

Acknowledgments

Travis, your patience and attentiveness have been instrumental in nurturing my spiritual growth. Your sincere belief in me serves as a daily reminder to persevere and embrace all that lies within. I'm profoundly grateful for your love, guidance, and—above all—your friendship.

Greene boys, your encouragement fuels my passion to continue to obey the Lord's instruction. I treasure each of you!

To my remarkable parents, Cynthia and Willie Ware, and Dr. Yaw Gyamfi: Your influence on my life has been immense. I see reflections of the best of you within me. I'm forever indebted to you for anchoring my faith in Jesus and instilling in me the courage to dream big. Mama Greene, you jumped right in to further these efforts, and I'm so grateful for you!

To my beloved spiritual parents, pastors Matthew and Mona Thompson: Your passion and dedication to the Lord ignite a fire within me to pursue and maintain close communion with Him. Your example of steadfast faithfulness serves as a well of inspiration.

To my mentor, therapist, spiritual guide, and confidant—Dr. Anita: Our journey together has only just begun, yet your commitment to pour into my life has already left an indelible mark. I am forever changed by your investment in me.

To the exceptional team at Nelson Books, especially my editors Janet Talbert and Natalie Nyquist, and all the talented individuals who contributed to the completion of this devotional. Your expertise and support have been invaluable.

To my literary agent, Lisa, and attorney, Denise: Your backing means the world to me.

To my collaborator, Danielle Butler: Your dedication and genuine effort to understand my voice and vision have made our collaboration truly remarkable. I eagerly anticipate our future endeavors together.

To my dear faith child, Jahniyah: Your unwavering support and sacrificial dedication to seeing God's vision for my life come to fruition fill me with a thankfulness that's beyond words.

To my DrJG/Forward City Team: Your tireless commitment and unwavering support ensure that Travis and I can offer our best to the world in every aspect. Thank you!

To the Permission Banner and Forward Family: You are my tribe, and your love and support are cherished deeply! May this devotional bring blessings to each of you.

Notes

1. Children's Bureau, "The Importance of Father Daughter Relationships," All4Kids *News* (blog), June 12, 2019, https://www.all4kids.org/news/blog/the-importance-of-father-daughter-relationships.

2. "Ranchi Man Celebrates Daughter's Return After Divorce," *Times of India*, October 25, 2023, https://timesofindia.indiatimes.com/etimes/trending/ranchi-man-celebrates-daughters-return-after-divorce/articleshow/104655203.cms.

3. Ellipses and brackets in the original transcript. Hermond Norwood, "Fountain Hughes," March 1, 2009, in *Voices from the Days of Slavery: Stories, Songs and Memories*, produced by the Library of Congress, podcast, streaming MP3, 18:15, https://www.loc.gov/podcasts/slavenarratives/podcast_hughes.html.

4. James Baldwin, *Fifty Famous People: A Book of Short Stories* (New York: American Book Company, 1912), 24–27.

5. Anita Phillips, *The Garden Within: Where the War with Your Emotions Ends and Your Most Powerful Life Begins* (Nashville: Thomas Nelson, 2023).

6. Valorie Burton, "5 Things Happy People Do Every Day," Valorie Burton (website), accessed February 8, 2024, https://valorieburton.com/5-things-happy-people-every-day/.

7. Lee Jussim, "Self-Fulfilling Prophecy," *Encyclopedia Britannica*, last updated December 22, 2023, https://www.britannica.com/topic/self-fulfilling-prophecy.

About the Author

Dr. Jacqueline Gyamfi Greene is an author, dentist, and co-pastor of Forward City Church. She embodies a fusion of traditional Southern values and Ghanaian heritage. Her latest book, *Permission to Live Free*, testifies to her commitment to empowering individuals in embracing their God-created authenticity. She is married to renowned gospel recording artist Travis Greene, and together they nurture three sons: David Jace (10), Travis Joshua (6), and Jonathan Judah Willie (5).